Contents

Page 2	Order of Operations
Page 3	Probability
Pages 4 & 5	Negative Numbers
Pages 6, 7 & 8	Handling Data
Pages 9 & 10	Area of a Triangle
Page 11	Long Division
Pages 12 & 13	Algebra
Pages 14 & 15	Ratio
Pages 16 & 17	Index Numbers
Page 18	Linear Equations
Page 19	Parallel Lines
Pages 20 & 21	Quadrilaterals
Pages 22 & 23	Decimals, Fractions, Percentages
Pages 24 & 25	Scatter Diagrams
Page 26	Angles in Polygons
Pages 27 & 28	Enlargements
Pages 29, 30 & 31	Circles
Page 32	Linear Patterns
Pages 33 & 34	Mappings
Page 35	Pie Charts
Pages 36 & 37	Class Intervals
Pages 38 & 39	Trial and Improvement
Pages 40 & 41	Equations of Lines
Page 42	Probability Again
Pages 43 & 44	More Ratio
Page 45	More Algebra
Pages 46, 47 & 48	Mental Arithmetic Practice
Page 49	Useful Mathematical Information

Order of Operations

Question: "Add three to four lots of two."   3 + 4 x 2

The **four lots of two** is worked out first, **before adding the three** ....

Answer: 3 + 8 = 11

As you can see, the multiplication is done before the addition.

Answer the following questions. Remember to work out the multiplication parts first.

(a) 6 x 7 + 3 =   (b) 14 + 3 x 2 =   (c) 4 x 3 + 8 x 5 =   (d) 9 + 9 x 9 =

Sometimes we need to work out the addition first .... so we use **brackets**:

Question: "Add three to four then multiply by two."   (3 + 4) x 2

Three add four equals seven. Seven multiplied by two is fourteen.

Answer: (3 + 4) x 2 = 14

Answer the following questions. Remember to work out the brackets parts first.

(e) 6 x (7 + 3) =   (f) (14 + 3) x 2 =   (g) 4 x (3 + 8) =   (h) (9 + 9) x 9 =

To remember the correct order of operations we use this as a clue: **B O D M A S**

Brackets   **O**f   **D**ivide **M**ultiply   **A**dd   **S**ubtract
            whichever is written first   whichever is written first

---

Examples: (1) $6 + \frac{1}{2}$ of 20   This question has an addition sign and an 'of'. In BODMAS an 'of' comes before an add so we must work out half of 20 before adding the 6.

$$6 + \tfrac{1}{2} \text{ of } 20 = 6 + 10 = 16$$

(2) 3 x 4 – 16 ÷ 8   Here we have a multiplication sign, a subtraction sign and a division sign, so we work out 3 x 4 and 16 ÷ 8 before we do the subtraction.

$$3 \times 4 - 16 \div 8 = 12 - 2 = 10$$

Now try these:

(i) 20 – 2 x 7 =   (j) (2 + 3) x (6 – 4) =   (k) 3 x (9 – 4) – 5 + 1 =   (l) $35 - 4 \times \tfrac{1}{2}$ of 10 =

Probability

The probability of an event happening is given by:

$$\frac{\text{the number of favourable outcomes}}{\text{the total number of outcomes}}$$

This example might help you:

Question: What is the probability of getting a multiple of 3 when rolling a die?

Solution: **3** and **6** are the only **multiples of 3** out of the six numbers 1, 2, 3, 4, 5, 6 ....

.... there are **two** 'favourable' outcomes out of a total of **six** possible outcomes.

So, the probability of getting a multiple of 3 is: **2 out of 6**

We write this as follows: P (a multiple of 3) = $\frac{2}{6}$

...... and we can simplify the answer: P (a multiple of 3) = $\frac{2}{6} = \frac{1}{3}$

This answer is not surprising because if you did roll a die a large number of times you would expect about a third of the outcomes to be a multiple of 3.

The smallest probability is when something will never happen.
For example, with an ordinary die it is impossible to roll a seven: P (rolling a 7) = $\frac{0}{6} = 0$

The largest probability is when something will always happen.
For example, with an ordinary die you will always roll a number which is less than 7:

P (rolling a number less than 7) = $\frac{6}{6} = 1$

Answer the following questions:

(1) For a normal six-sided die write down:

 (a) **P (odd number)**   (b) **P (a number greater than 4)**   (c) **P (a prime number)**

(2) If you roll a die 30 times:

 (a) **How many times would you expect a 2 to come up?**

 (b) **How many times would you expect an even number to come up?**

Arithmetic with Negative Numbers

Negative numbers are sometimes written like this: -2
..... and sometimes like this: ⁻2

Positive numbers are usually just written like this: 4
..... but sometimes like this: ⁺4

When adding a positive number to another positive number you get an answer which is bigger than the number you started with:

⁺6 + ⁺2 = ⁺8

Adding a negative number does the reverse and you get an answer which is smaller than the number you started with:

⁺6 + ⁻2 = ⁺4

When you subtract a positive number from a positive number you get an answer which is smaller than the number you started with:

⁺6 – ⁺2 = ⁺4

When you subtract a negative number from a positive number you get an answer which is bigger than the number you started with:

⁺6 – ⁻2 = ⁺8

You may find this quite confusing!

These rules will help you:

> **The first number in the sum tells you where to start on the number line.**
>
> **The second number tells you how many spaces to move.**
>
> **If the two signs in the middle are the same, you move up.**
>
> **If you have one of each sign you move down.**

Adding and Subtracting with Negative Numbers

You may wish to use this number line to help you to answer the questions below.

⁻23 ⁻22 ⁻21 ⁻20 ⁻19 ⁻18 ⁻17 ⁻16 ⁻15 ⁻14 ⁻13 ⁻12 ⁻11 ⁻10 ⁻9 ⁻8 ⁻7 ⁻6 ⁻5 ⁻4 ⁻3 ⁻2 ⁻1 0 ⁺1 ⁺2 ⁺3 ⁺4 ⁺5 ⁺6 ⁺7 ⁺8 ⁺9 ⁺10

(a) $^+7 - {^-3}$ (b) $^+10 + {^-4}$ (c) $^-6 + {^-3}$ (d) $^-8 + {^+2}$

(e) $^+10 - {^+6}$ (f) $^-5 - {^-5}$ (g) $^-9 - {^+3}$ (h) $^+7 - {^-6}$

(i) $^+11 + {^-9}$ (j) $^-6 + {^+6}$ (k) $^-20 - {^+3}$ (l) $^-15 - {^-7}$

Multiplying and Dividing with Negative Numbers

Multiplying and dividing both use these rules:

"Two negatives make a positive"

"One of each sign makes a negative"

Think about the rules as you look at these examples:

$^+4 \times {^+5} = {^+20}$ $^+20 \div {^+5} = {^+4}$

$^-4 \times {^-5} = {^+20}$ $^+20 \div {^-5} = {^-4}$

$^-4 \times {^+5} = {^-20}$ $^-20 \div {^+5} = {^-4}$

$^+4 \times {^-5} = {^-20}$ $^-20 \div {^-5} = {^+4}$

Use the rules to help you to answer these questions:

(m) $^-6 \times {^-7}$ (n) $^-8 \times {^+12}$ (o) $^+11 \times {^+11}$ (p) $^+9 \times {^-6}$

(q) $^-8 \times {^-7}$ (r) $^+12 \times {^-5}$ (s) $^-84 \div {^+7}$ (t) $^+36 \div {^-6}$

(u) $^+108 \div {^+12}$ (v) $^-72 \div {^-9}$ (w) $^+72 \div {^-6}$ (x) $^-49 \div {^-7}$

Handling Data: The Mean

The mean is another piece of information that can be found from a set of data. Finding the mean can help you to understand the data better.

Range, mode and median were all looked at in Book One.

The mean is what most people call "the average" although mode and median are also types of average.

To work out the mean:

        Step 1:   **add all the data together**

        Step 2:   **divide by the number of pieces of data**

This example may help you:

    Calculate the mean of   6, 19, 8, 11, 17, 11

There are six numbers here ...
.... so we add them together and divide by 6

$$(6 + 19 + 8 + 11 + 17 + 11) \div 6$$

$$72 \div 6 = 12$$

.... so the mean of of this set of data is 12

Answer the following questions:

(1) Find the mean of the following sets of data:

    (a)   20, 24, 29, 23, 24   (b)   7, 1, 9, 5, 0, 6, 9, 8, 9

    (c)   12, 15, 17, 20   (d)   112, 115, 117, 120

(2) The contents of six matchboxes are: 51, 49, 54, 53, 54, 51
What is the mean number of matches in a box?

(3) In six cricket matches: player A scores 12, 28, 25, 39, 40 and 27
                            player B scores 19, 53, 0, 62, 29 and 8

    (a)   Find the mean score for player A. (b)   Find the mean score for player B.

    (c)   Find the range for player A.   (d)   Find the range for player B.

    (e)   Which of the two is the more consistent player?

Handling Data: Understanding Diagrams

This graph can be used to convert between litres and gallons.

The dotted line shows how 12 litres converts to 2.6 gallons.

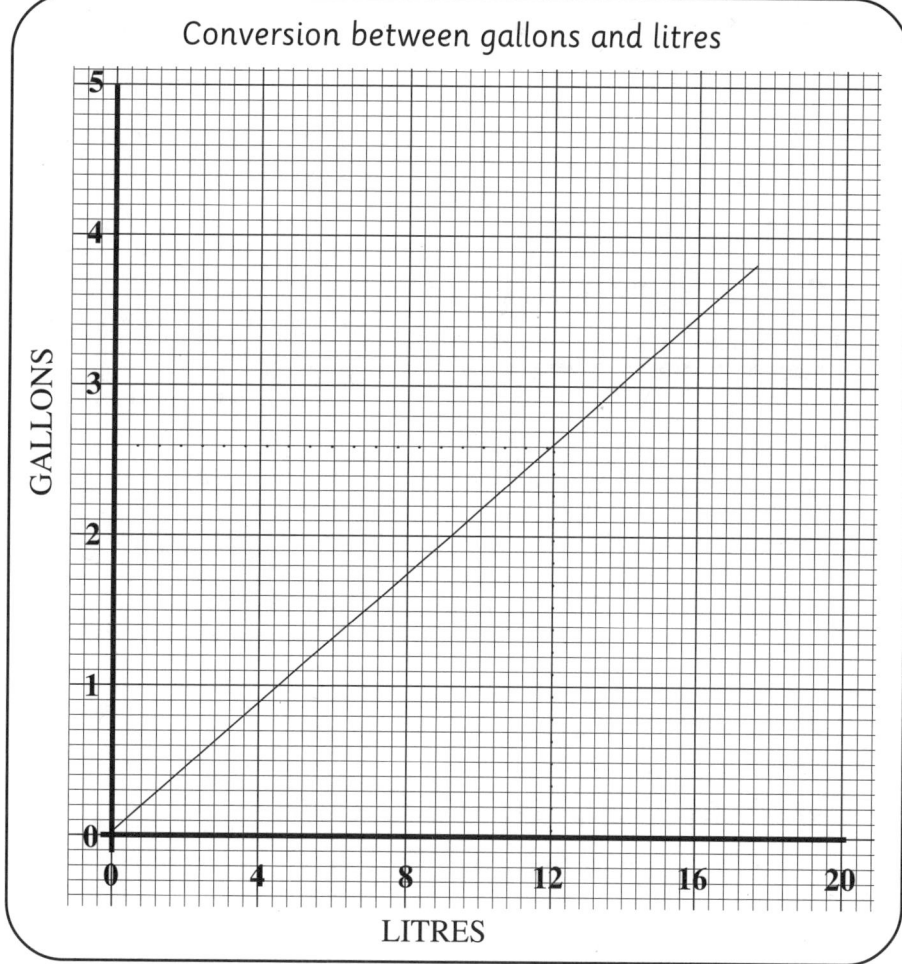

Conversion between gallons and litres

Use the graph to change these four quantities:

(a) 6 l =   galls

(b) 17 l =   galls

(c) 1 gall =   l

(d) 3.5 galls =   l

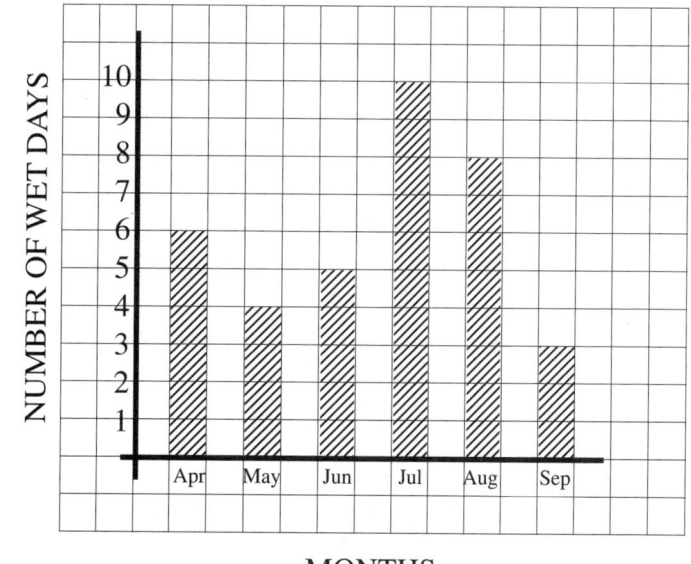

The bar chart shows the number of wet days in each month over a six month period.

You can see, for instance, that June had five wet days.

Look at the bar chart to find the answers to these questions:

(e) Which month has most wet days?

(f) How many wet days were there altogether over the six months?

(g) What was the mean number of wet days per month?

7

Handling Data: More Diagrams

This pie chart shows the results when 60 people were asked their favourite sport.

If we were asked how many people liked netball best we could work it out like this:

There are 360° in a circle.

The angle shown for netball is 30°.

$$360° \div 30° = 12$$

..... so netball is represented by $\frac{1}{12}$ of the circle.

$\frac{1}{12}$ of 60 people is 5.

5 people like netball best.

Answer the following questions:

(a) How many people preferred basketball?

(b) How many people preferred hockey?

(c) How many people preferred rugby?

(d) How many people did not choose football as their favourite sport?

---

90 people were asked how many books they read during the summer holiday.

The results are displayed on this pie chart.

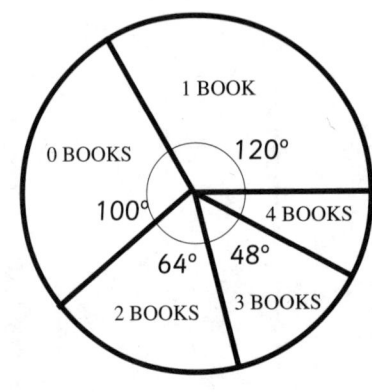

How many people read:

(e) No books?   (f) 1 book?   (g) 2 books?   (h) 3 books?   (i) 4 books?

Area of a Triangle

We can call this triangle '**triangle ABC**'.
We sometimes write 'triangle ABC' like this: △ABC

The line BC is known as the base of △ABC.
If we draw a perpendicular from the vertex A to
the line BC this gives us the height of △ABC.

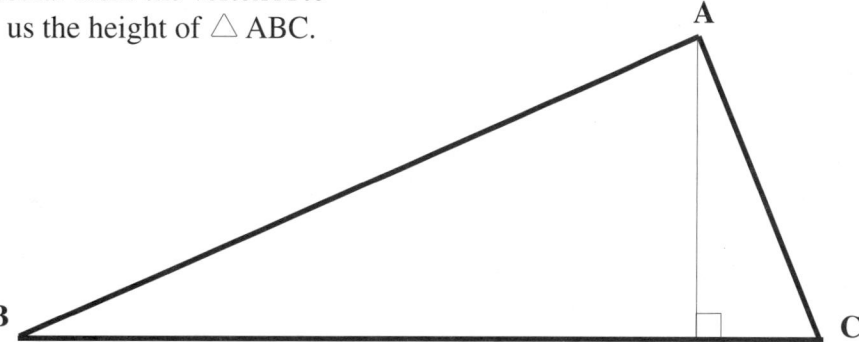

If you measure you will find that the base is 11 cm long.
The height is 4 cm.

You can find the area using the formula $\frac{1}{2}$ **x base x height**.

So, the area of △ABC = $\frac{1}{2}$ x 11 x 4.

$\frac{1}{2}$ x 11 x 4 = 22

The answer must be given in square centimetres: Area of △ABC = 22 cm²

**Measure the base and the height of each of the triangles below.
Use your measurements to calculate the area of each one.
You will need to use this formula:**

Area of a triangle = $\frac{1}{2}$ x base x height.

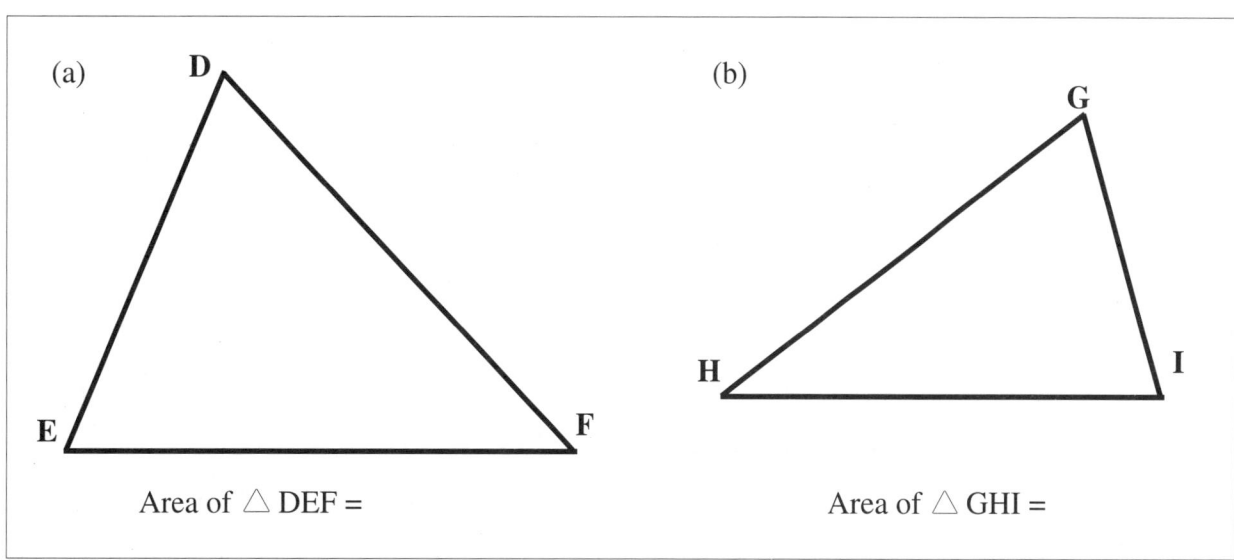

(a) Area of △DEF =

(b) Area of △GHI =

9

Area of a Triangle

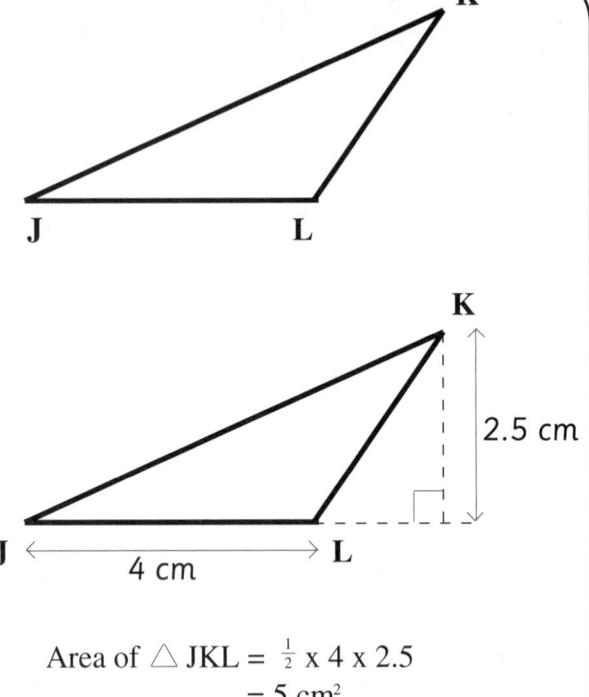

This is an obtuse triangle.
It is called an obtuse triangle because one of its angles is more than 90°.

We could find its area by turning the book around so that the base of the triangle is the line JK ....

.... or we can extend the line JL until we can draw a perpendicular to K:

Area of △ JKL = $\frac{1}{2}$ x 4 x 2.5
= 5 cm²

Find the area of each of the triangles below.
You may need to turn the book around.
You may need to draw the triangles and, for each one, extend one of its lines until you can find its perpendicular height.

You will need to use this formula:

Area of a triangle = $\frac{1}{2}$ x base x height.

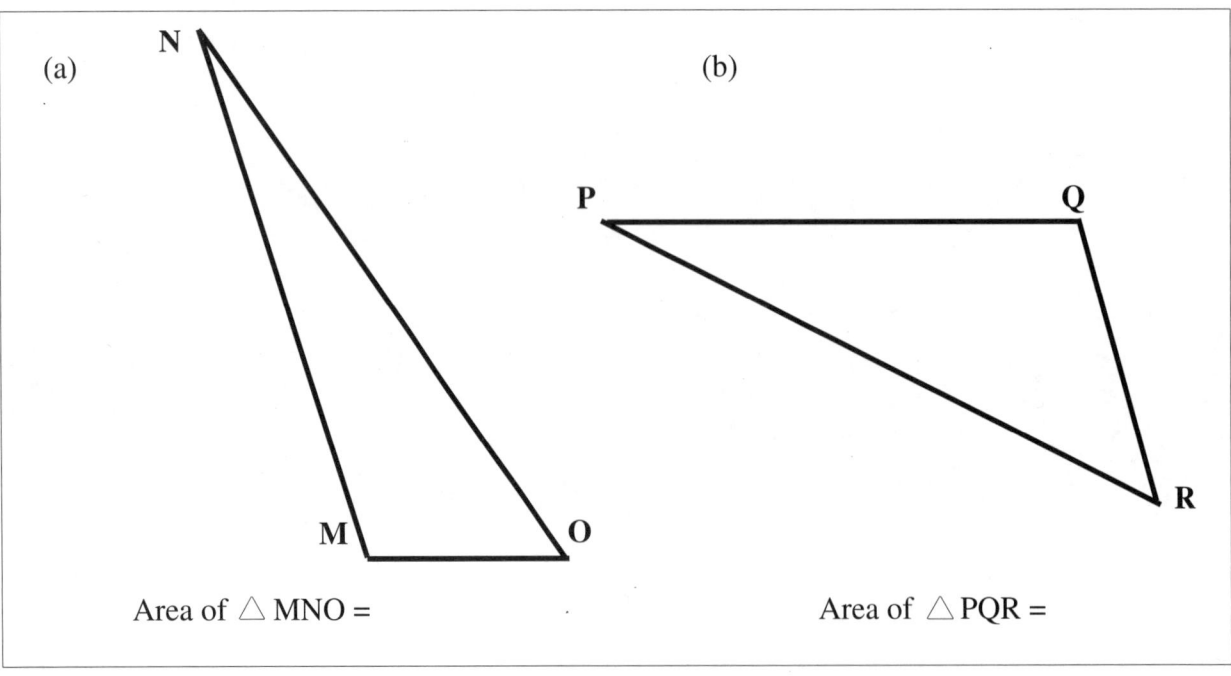

(a) Area of △ MNO =

(b) Area of △ PQR =

10

Long Division

Long division is used when dividing by a number larger than 10, without a calculator.

The method is similar to ordinary division but, because of the larger numbers, we write down the working out as part of the sum:

Example   782 ÷ 23

⬇

23)782

As 23 is close to 20 ask yourself:
Does 20 divide into 7? - No
Does 20 divide into 78? - yes 3 x 20 = 60
So now work out 3 x 23:
3 x 23 = 69

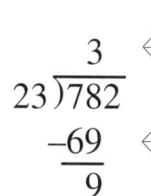

⬇

```
      3
23)782
   -69
     9
```

We subtract the 69 from the 78 to leave 9

⬇

```
      3
23)782
    69↓
    92
```

Now bring down the next digit and ask yourself:
Does 20 divide into 92? Yes 4 x 20 = 80
So now work out 4 x 23
4 x 23 = 92

⬇

```
     34
23)782
    69
    92
    92
     0 remainder
```

...... so 782 ÷ 23 = 34, with no remainder.

Now try these:

(a) 817 ÷ 19   (b) 868 ÷ 31   (c) 966 ÷ 42

(d) 884 ÷ 26   (e) 6975 ÷ 31   (f) 6552 ÷ 28

Algebra

Section A Substituting numbers for letters:

If $a = 6$ and $b = 9$ ..... then $a + b = 6 + 9$
$= 15$

$2a = 2 \times 6$ ($2a$ is short for $2 \times a$)
$= 12$

$ab = 6 \times 9$ (ab is short for $a \times b$)
$= 54$

$a^2 = 36$ (a^2 is short for $a \times a$)

Answer the following questions where $a = 6$ and $b = 9$:

(a) $2a + b =$ (b) $b^2 =$ (c) $2b + 10 =$ (d) $4a + 4b =$ (e) $4(a + b)$ (f) $4ab$

Section B Collecting like terms:

Even if you do not know the value of a letter, an expression can sometimes be simplified.
Letters which are the same can be collected together.
Look **carefully** at these examples:

$2x + 3x = 5x$

$2x + 6y + 3x - 2y = 5x + 4y$ (because $2x + 3x = 5x$ and $6y - 2y = 4y$)

$2x + 6 + 3x - 2 = 5x + 4$ (we gather the x terms together and the ordinary numbers together)

$2x + 6xy + 3x - 2xy = 5x + 4xy$ (an xy term is different to an x term or a y term)

$2xy + 3yx = 5xy$ ($x \times y$ is the same as $y \times x$)

Simplify these:

(g) $6c - 4c + 7c =$ (h) $10d - 7 - 3d + 16 =$ (i) $3e^2 + 8e^2 =$

(j) $11f + 3g - 6f - 6g =$ (k) $3h + 2hi + 11hi - 3h =$ (l) $30jk - 16kj + 2kj - 11jk =$

More Algebra

Section C   Multiplying out a bracket:

In Section A on page 12, you should have found that questions (d) and (e) had the same answer:

4a + 4b is the same as 4(a + b).

Look carefully at 4(a + b):

$$4(a + b)$$

The 4 on the outside of the brackets multiplies both the a <u>and</u> the b on the inside.

The 4 multiplies b (4 x b) and a (4 x a).

.... so 4(a + b) = 4a + 4b

Here are some more examples.
Examining them carefully will help you with the questions on this page.

$$4(2a + 3b) = 8a + 12b$$
(4 x 2a, 4 x 3b)

$$4(2a - 3b) = 8a - 12b$$
(4 x 2a, 4 x ⁻3b)

$$⁻4(2a + 3b) = ⁻8a - 12b$$
(⁻4 x 2a, ⁻4 x 3b)

$$⁻4(2a - 3b) = ⁻8a + 12b$$
(⁻4 x 2a, ⁻4 x ⁻3b)

This one could be confusing but don't forget that two negatives make a positive.

Multiply out these brackets:

(a) $6(3m + 7n)$

(b) $8(5p - 8q)$

(c) $⁻3(9r + s)$

(d) $7(9t - 9)$

(e) $⁻4(⁻11u - 8v)$

(f) $⁻9(12x - 11y)$

Ratio

A ratio is a way of comparing quantities.

It is written as numbers separated by a colon.

For example, if Stuart has £1 and James has £4 then the amount of money that Stuart has compared to James can be written as **the unitary ratio 1:4**

The order <u>does</u> matter. As we wrote Stuart's name first we must write the ratio as 1:4 (If we were to write 4:1 this would mean that Stuart has four times as much as James)

Look at another example:

Samantha and Joanne also have money in the ratio 1:4

This does not tell you how much either girl has, just that Joanne has four times as much as Samantha ......

.... but, if you are told that Samantha has £3,
you can then work out that Joanne has £12.

Answer the following questions about ratios.

(a) The amount that Andrew and Billy earn is in the ratio 1:2.
If Andrew earns £325 in a week, how much does Billy earn?

(b) Claire and Diane pay for a bag of sweets in the ratio 1:3.
If Diane pays 75p, how much does Claire pay?

(c) A model car and the real thing are in the ratio 1:20.

    (i) If the model is 20cm long, how long is the real car?

    (ii) If the real car has windscreen wipers that are 50cm long, how long will they be on the model?

(d) In a cake recipe the ratio of sugar to flour is 1:4.

    (i) If 50g of sugar are used, what weight of flour is needed?

    (ii) A larger cake is made for a party and 460g of flour are used. How many grams of sugar are needed?

More Ratios

We use ratios when we are looking at scales on maps and plans.

Answer these questions about a scale plan of a classroom, drawn to a scale of 1:60.

(a) How long is the classroom on the plan?

(b) How long is the actual classroom?

(c) How wide is the classroom on the plan?

(d) How wide is the actual classroom?

(e) Both bookcases on the plan measure 20mm by 5mm. What would be the dimensions of the real bookcase?

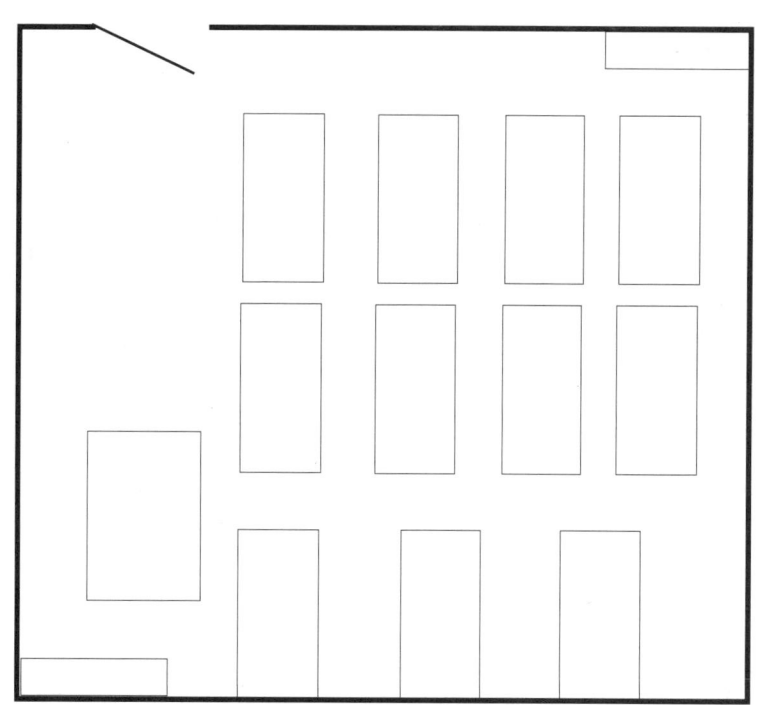

If you know two quantities you can write them as a ratio straight away:

For example, there are 15 sweets in a small box and 60 sweets in a large box.
The ratio of sweets in the small box to the large box is **15:60**.
However, because 15 divides into 60 four times (60 ÷ 15 = 4) we can say that the large box holds four times as many sweets as the small box ....
.... so the ratio of sweets in the small box to the large box is **1:4**.

We can see that the ratio 15:60 can be written as the ratio 1:4.

1:4 is called a **unitary ratio**, because one of the numbers is **1**.

Give ratios as your answers to the questions below:

(f) A small coach carries 21 people and a large coach carries 42. What is the ratio of the number of people carried on the small coach to the number carried on the large coach?

(g) Give your answer to question (f) as a unitary ratio.

(h) An individual packet of cereals weighs 20g and a medium size packet weighs 340g. What is the ratio of the weight of the small packet to the weight of the large packet?

(i) Give your answer to question (h) as a unitary ratio.

Rules of Index Numbers

> The meaning of index numbers was covered on page 16 of *Maths for Ages 11-12*

Evaluate the following questions, using a calculator where necessary:

(a) $2^3 \times 2^2 =$

(b) $2^5 =$

(c) $2^6 \times 2^3 =$

(d) $2^9 =$

(e) $3^4 \times 3^2 =$

(f) $3^6 =$

(g) $5^2 \times 5^3 =$

(h) $5^5 =$

You should see a pattern to the answers in these pairs of questions.

The pattern shows you how to simplify powers of the same number that are being multiplied.

Look at another example:

$$4^3 \times 4^2 \text{ simplifies to } 4^5$$

Notice that the index numbers 3 and 2 are added together to give the index number 5.

This works because $4^3 \times 4^2$ means $(4 \times 4 \times 4) \times (4 \times 4)$ ....

.... and the short way of writing this is 4^5.

This is the first rule of index numbers.

Note: on a calculator the power button looks like x^y or y^x

... so to find 4^5 you need to press these buttons: 4 x^y 5 $=$

Simplify the following, then use your calculator to find the answer.

The first one is done for you.

(i) $5^3 \times 5^2 \times 5^4 = 5^9 = 1953125$

(j) $6^3 \times 6^4 =$ =

(k) $4^2 \times 4^2 \times 4^3 =$ =

(l) $2^4 \times 2^5 \times 2^5 =$ =

(m) $10^2 \times 10^2 \times 10^2 =$ =

More Rules of Index Numbers

The first ten powers of two are shown in this table:

$2^1 = 2$

$2^2 = 4$

$2^3 = 8$

$2^4 = 16$

$2^5 = 32$

$2^6 = 64$

$2^7 = 128$

$2^8 = 256$

$2^9 = 512$

$2^{10} = 1024$

Use the results from the table to work out the answers to the following questions:

(a) $2^9 \div 2^5 =$

(b) $2^4 =$

(c) $2^8 \div 2^3 =$

(d) $2^5 =$

(e) $2^8 \div 2^2 =$

(f) $2^6 =$

(g) $2^{10} \div 2^7 =$

(h) $2^3 =$

Again, there is a pattern to the answers in these pairs of questions.

The pattern shows you how to simplify powers of the same number that are being divided.

Look at another example:

$$2^9 \div 2^5 \text{ simplifies to } 2^4$$

Notice that the index numbers 9 and 5 are subtracted to give the index number 4.

This is the second rule of index numbers.

Simplify the following, then use your calculator to find the answer.

The first one is done for you.

(i) $4^6 \div 4^2 = 4^4 = 256$

(j) $5^{10} \div 5^7 = \quad =$

(k) $9^{15} \div 9^{12} = \quad =$

17

Linear Equations

Think of a number ...... add 2 .... subtract 2 ......
...... you have, of course, got back to the number you started with.

We say that subtracting two is the **inverse** of adding two.
It has the opposite effect and "undoes" the add two.

subtracting undoes adding
adding undoes subtracting

multiplying undoes dividing
dividing undoes multiplying

We use these facts when we are **solving** equations (finding the value of the letter).

We treat an equation like a balance and **do the same thing to both sides** so it will still balance.

Look at this equation: $2x = 16$

Here we want to find the value of the x. On the left side we have $2x$ which means $2 \times x$.

If we divide both sides by 2 we will be able to "undo" the $2 \times x$, leaving the x on its own.

$2x = 16$ → divide both sides by 2 → $x = 8$

We have solved the equation because we have found that $x = 8$.

More examples:

(i) $\dfrac{x}{4} = 16$

$x = 64$ We have multiplied both sides by 4 to undo the 'divide by 4'.

(ii) $3x + 2 = 20$
$3x = 18$ We have subtracted 2 from both sides.
$x = 6$ We have divided by 3 on both sides.

(iii) $4x - 7 = 2x + 3$
$2x - 7 = 3$ We have subtracted $2x$ from both sides.
$2x = 10$ We have added 7 to both sides.
$x = 5$ We have divided both sides by 2.

(a) $6x = 42$ (b) $8 = \dfrac{x}{2}$ (c) $3 + x = 17$ (d) $x - 8 = 24$ (e) $3x + 7 = 22$

(f) $5x - 8 = 37$ (g) $6x - 2 = 4x + 20$ (h) $4x + 16 = 7x - 5$

Parallel Lines

Transversal Lines

A line that crosses a pair of parallel lines is called a **transversal**.

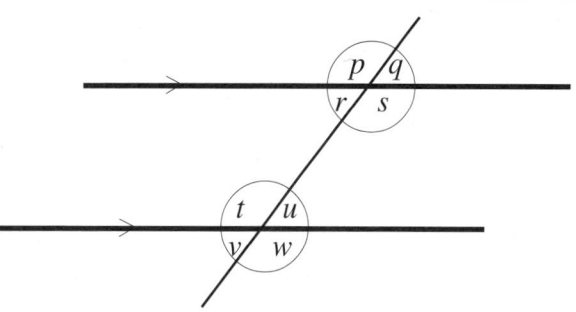

Corresponding Angles

Angles that are in similar positions are called **corresponding angles**.

In this diagram:
p and t are corresponding angles
q and u are corresponding angles
r and v are corresponding angles

(a) Which others are corresponding angles?

Interior Angles

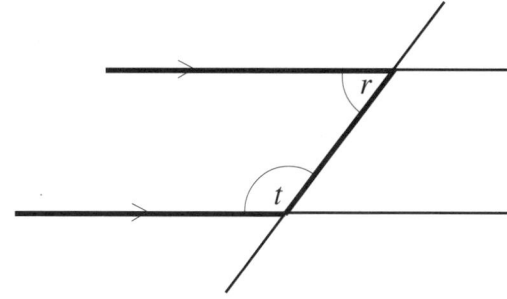   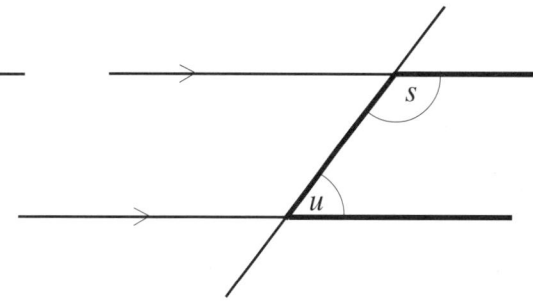

Angles r and t are called **interior angles**.
Angles r and t add up to 180°.

Angles s and u are also **interior angles**.
Angles s and u add up to 180°.

Alternate Angles

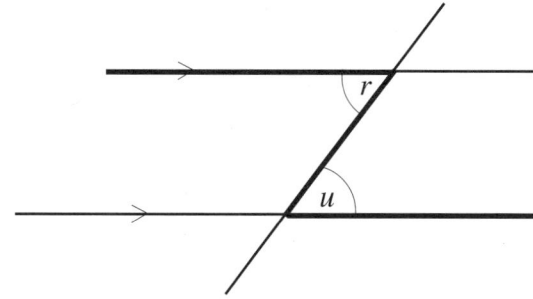   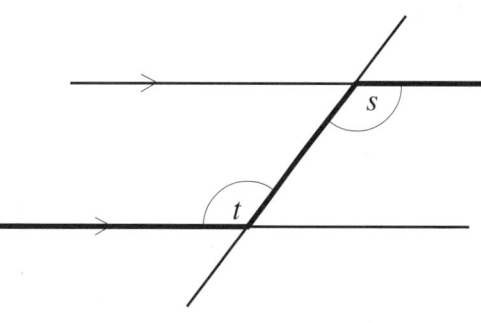

Angles r and u are called **alternate angles**.
Angle r is the same size as angle u.

Angles s and t are also **alternate angles**.
Angle s is the same size as angle t.

Angles around Parallel Lines, continued

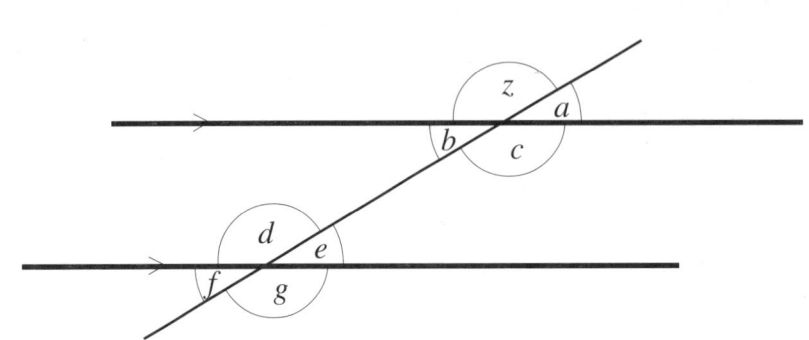

Angle z is equal to 150°

Use that information, and the rules on page 19, to work out the sizes of all the other angles.

Quadrilaterals

Any four sided shape is a quadrilateral.

There are six different types of quadrilateral which have special features:

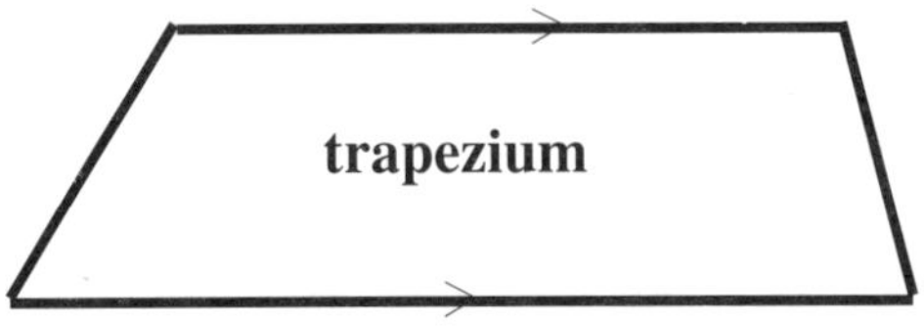

trapezium

The trapezium has one pair of sides which are parallel.

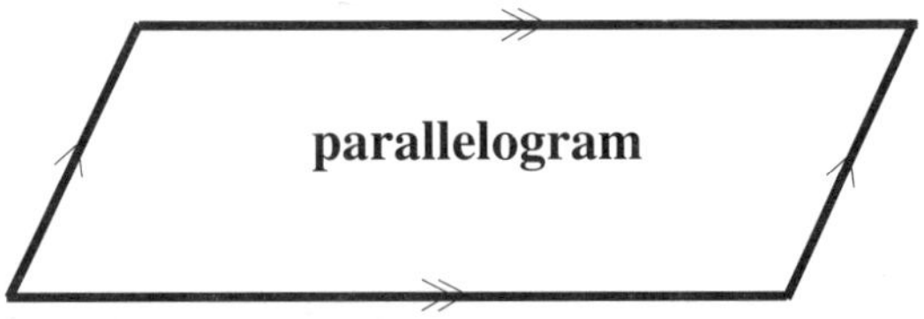

parallelogram

In the parallelogram both pairs of sides are parallel.

kite

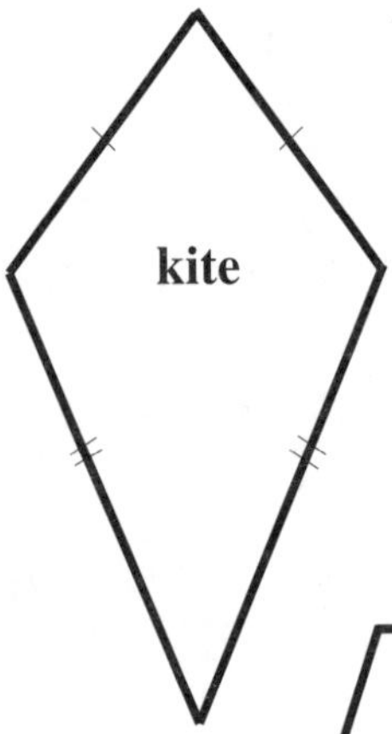

The kite has two pairs of adjoining sides which are equal in length.

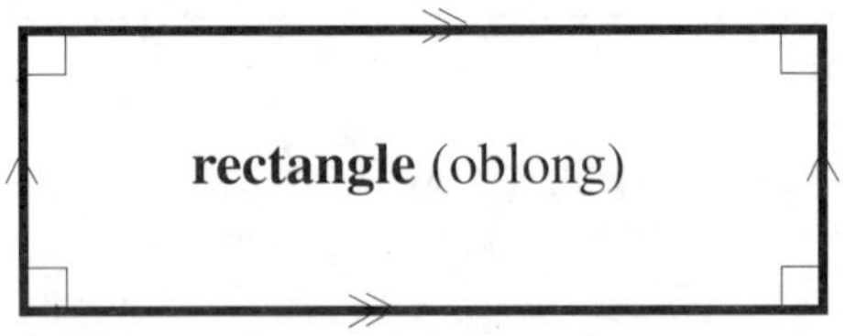

rectangle (oblong)

In the rectangle both pairs of sides are parallel and all corners are 90°.

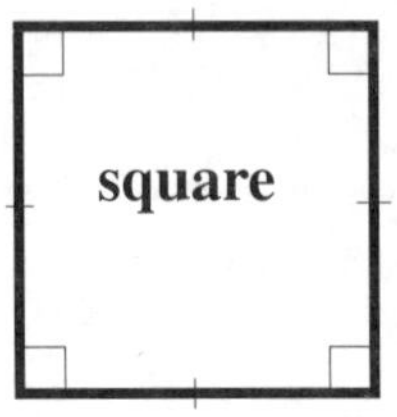

rhombus

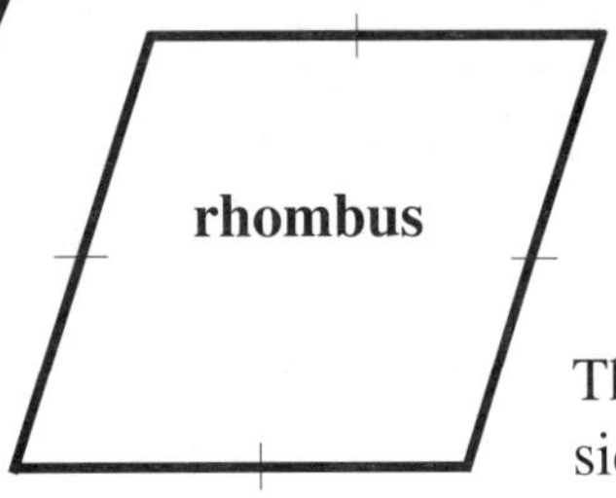

The rhombus has all sides equal in length.

square

In the square:
Both pairs of sides are parallel.
All sides are equal in length.
All corners are 90°.

20

Quadrilaterals, continued

If you look carefully at the shapes on page 20 you will see that:

Arrowheads are used to show parallel lines:

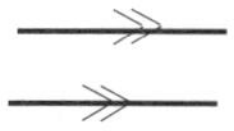

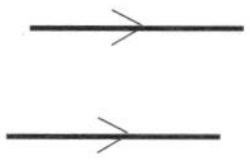

Dashes are used to show equal length lines:

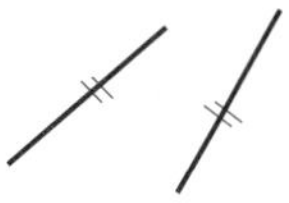

Notice as well that a square is a special type of rhombus:

A rhombus has four equal sides but a square has corners which are right angles.

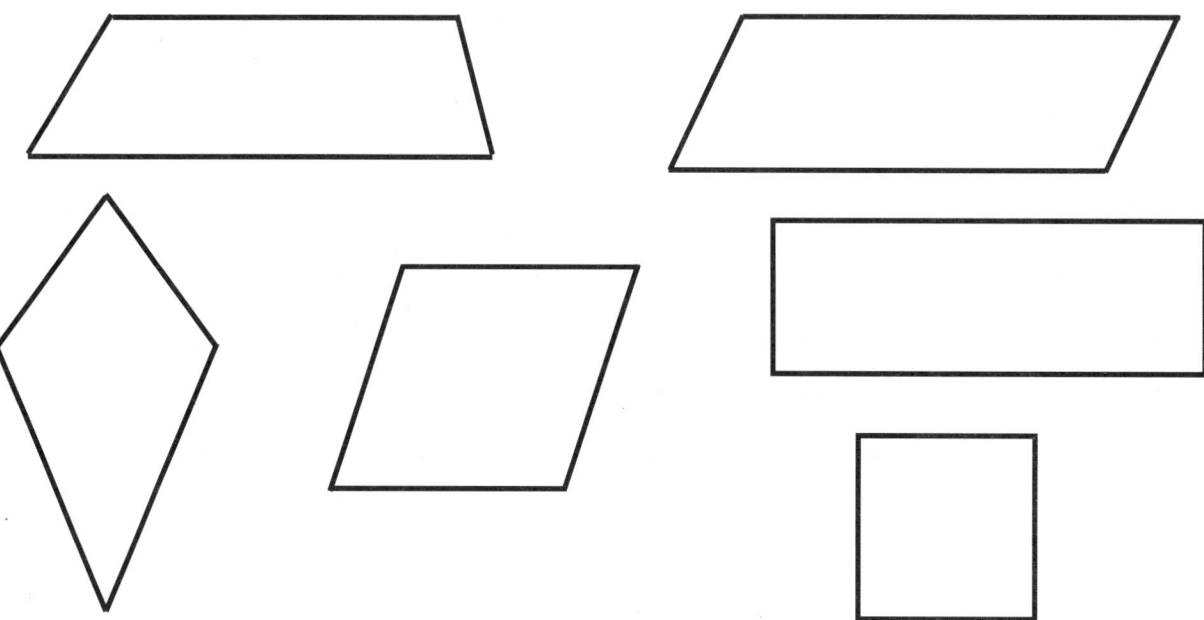

Draw an accurate copy of each of the six quadrilaterals.
Draw in both diagonals for each one.

Answer these questions about them:

(a) Which of the six shapes have both diagonals equal in length?

(b) In which of the six shapes are both the diagonals bisected?
  (**bisected** means cut exactly in half)

(c) In which of the six shapes do the diagonals bisect each corner?
  (measure carefully with a protractor)

(d) In which of the six shapes are the diagonals perpendicular?
  (**perpendicular** means they cross each other at 90°)

Decimals, Fractions, Percentages

In a test if someone gets a mark of $\frac{50}{100}$ we say that they have got fifty percent: 50%

We could also say that the person got half marks: $\frac{50}{100}$ is the same as $\frac{1}{2}$.

Of course, a half is the same as zero point five: $\frac{1}{2}$ is the same as 0·5.

.... so $\frac{50}{100} = \frac{1}{2} = 0·5 = 50\%$

To change a fraction to a decimal:
divide the top by the bottom .... $\frac{30}{50} = 0·6$ (30 ÷ 50 = 0·6)

To change a decimal to a percentage:
multiply by 100 ....   0·61 = 61%   (0·61 × 100)

To change a percentage to a fraction:
put the number over 100 and simplify (cancel down) .... $54\% = \frac{54}{100} = \frac{27}{50}$

To change a fraction to a percentage:
first change it to a decimal then change the decimal to a percentage.

Try these conversions:

(a) $\frac{16}{20} = 0\cdot$___

(b) 0·55 = ___%

(c) $36\% = \frac{}{100} = \frac{}{25}$

(d) 0·7 = ___%

(e) $\frac{24}{40} = 0\cdot$___

(f) $82\% = \frac{}{100} = \frac{}{}$

(g) $\frac{5}{8} =$ ___%

(h) 18% = 0·___

(i) $45\% = \frac{}{100} = \frac{}{}$

Fractions/Percentages of Another Quantity

If an item originally costs £10 but is increased to £11, we can express the increase as a fraction of the original amount:

The price has gone up by £1 compared to the original price of £10 so we say that the price has increased by $\frac{1}{10}$.

We could also express this as a percentage by changing this fraction to a decimal and multiplying by 100:

$$\frac{1}{10} = 0.1 \quad \ldots \quad 0.1 \times 100 = 10$$

$$\ldots \text{ so } \quad \frac{1}{10} = 0.1 = 10\%$$

The price of the item has increased by $\frac{1}{10}$ or 10%.

A decrease works in a similar way:

Original price £20 ... decrease by £1 to £19 ... The decrease is $\frac{1}{20}$ or 5%.

Copy out and complete the following table:

original amount	new amount	increase/decrease	fractional change	% change
25 kg	30 kg	increase 5 kg	$\frac{5}{25} = \frac{1}{5}$	20%
50 mm	45 mm			
£120		increase £30		
60 cl		decrease 18 cl		
80 p	92 p			
200 g			increase $\frac{1}{8}$	

Scatter Diagrams

A scatter diagram or scatter graph allows two pieces of data to be shown at the same time. For instance the height and weight of the ten Year 8 students shown in the table below could be displayed on a graph.

Person number:	1	2	3	4	5	6	7	8	9	10
Weight (kg):	47·2	43	40·6	41·5	48	44·4	51·8	49·8	44	43·3
Height (cm):	160	152	151	148	165	158	166	160	156	154

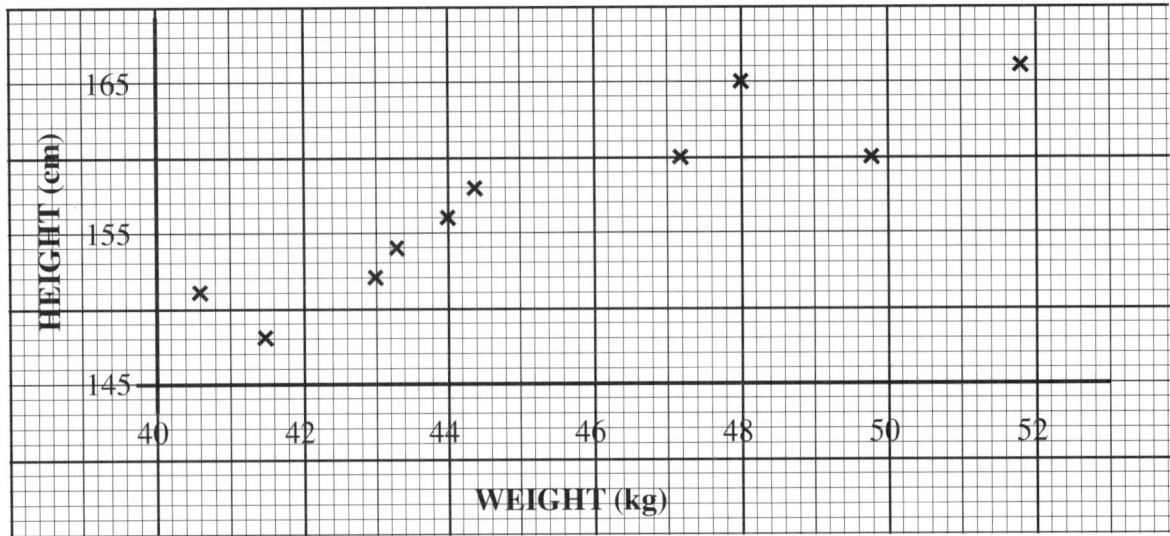

It can be seen from the graph that generally the heavier someone is, the taller they are. The points go from the bottom left to the top right because as one quantity increases so does the other. This is called **positive correlation**.

As the points are not too spread out, a **line of best fit** can be drawn in. This can be used to estimate the height or weight of other people. For example, someone who weighs 46 kg might be around 158.5 cm tall:

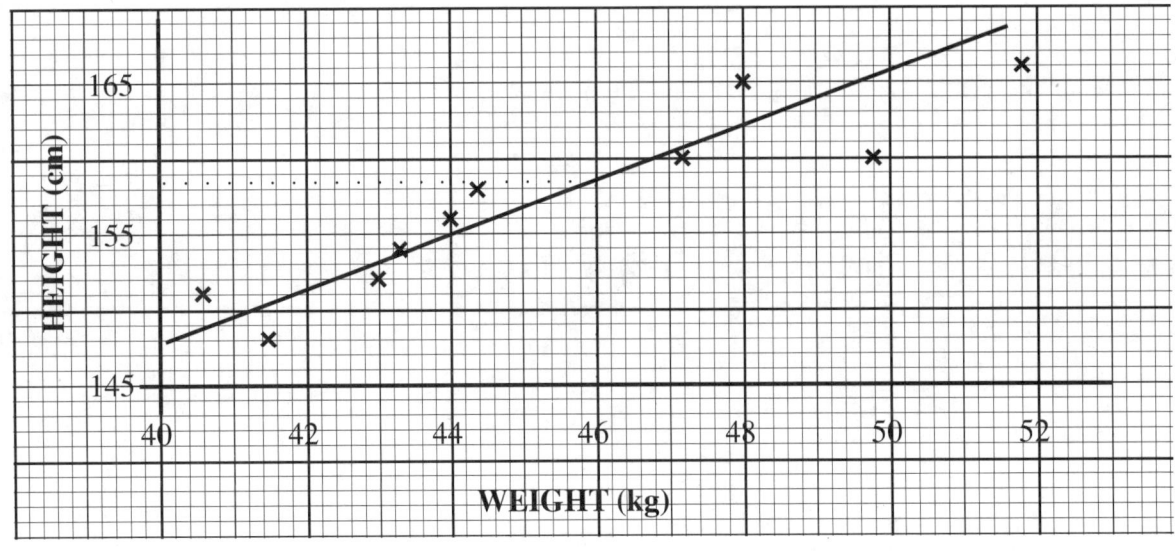

Removable Answer Section

Page 2   a 45   b 20   c 52   d 90   e 60   f 34   g 44   h 162   i 6   j 10   k 11   l 15

Page 3   (1)a $\frac{3}{6}=\frac{1}{2}$ b $\frac{2}{6}=\frac{1}{3}$ c $\frac{3}{6}=\frac{1}{2}$ (2)a 5 times   b 15 times

Page 5   a 10   b 6   c ⁻9   d ⁻6   e 4   f 0   g ⁻12   h 13   i 2   j 0   k ⁻23   l ⁻8
         m 42   n ⁻96   o 121   p ⁻54   q 56   r ⁻60   s ⁻12   t ⁻6   u 9   v 8   w ⁻12   x 7

Page 6   (1)a 24   b 6   c 16   d 116   (2) 52
         (3)a $28\frac{1}{2}$ b $28\frac{1}{2}$ c 28   d 62   e Player A

Page 7   a 1·3 galls   b 3·7 galls   c 4·6 l   d 16·2 l   e July   f 36   g 6

Page 8   a 10   b 15   c 10   d 40   e 25   f 30   g 16   h 12   i 7

Page 9   a $17\frac{1}{2}$ cm²   b 11·1 cm²

Page 10 a 9·8 cm²   b 12·2 cm²

Page 11 a 43   b 28   c 23   d 34   e 225   f 234

Page 12 a 21   b 81   c 28   d 60   e 60   f 216   g 9c   h 7d + 9
         i 11e²   j 5f – 3g   k 13hi   l 7jk

Page 13 a 18m + 42n   b 40p – 64q   c ⁻27r – 3s   d 63t – 63   e 44u + 32v   f ⁻108x + 99y

Page 14 a £650   b 25p   c(i) 400cm or 4m   (ii) $2\frac{1}{2}$ cm   d(i) 200g   (ii) 115g

Page 15 a 10cm   b 600cm or 6m   c 9cm   d 540cm or 5·4m
         e 1200mm or 1·2m by 300mm or 30cm   f 21:42   g 1:2   h 20:340   i 1:17

Page 16 a 32   b 32   c 512   d 512   e 729   f 729   g 3125   h 3125   i given
         j 6^7 = 279936   k 4^7 = 16384   l 2^{14} = 16384   m 10^6 = 1,000,000

Page 17 a 16   b 16   c 32   d 32   e 64   f 64   g 8   h 8   i given
         j 5^3 = 125   k 9^3 = 729

Page 18 a x = 7   b x = 16   c x = 14   d x = 32   e 3x = 15, x = 5   f 5x = 45, x = 9
         g 6x = 4x + 22   h 16 = 3x – 5
           2x =   22   21 = 3x
            x =   11   7 = x

Page 19   a s and w   Page 20   c = d = g = 150°   a = b = e = f = 30°

Page 21   a rectangle and square   b parallelogram, rhombus, rectangle and square

          c rhombus and square   d rhombus and square

Page 22   a 0·8   b 55%   c $\frac{36}{100} = \frac{9}{25}$ d 70%   e 0·6   f $\frac{82}{100} = \frac{41}{50}$ g 62·5%

          h 0·18   i $\frac{45}{100} = \frac{9}{20}$

Page 23   decrease 5mm $\frac{5}{50} = \frac{1}{10}$ 10%

          £150 $\frac{30}{120} = \frac{1}{4}$ 25%

          42cl $\frac{18}{60} = \frac{3}{10}$ 30%

          increase 12p $\frac{12}{80} = \frac{3}{20}$ 15%

          225g   increase 25g $12\frac{1}{2}\%$

Page 25

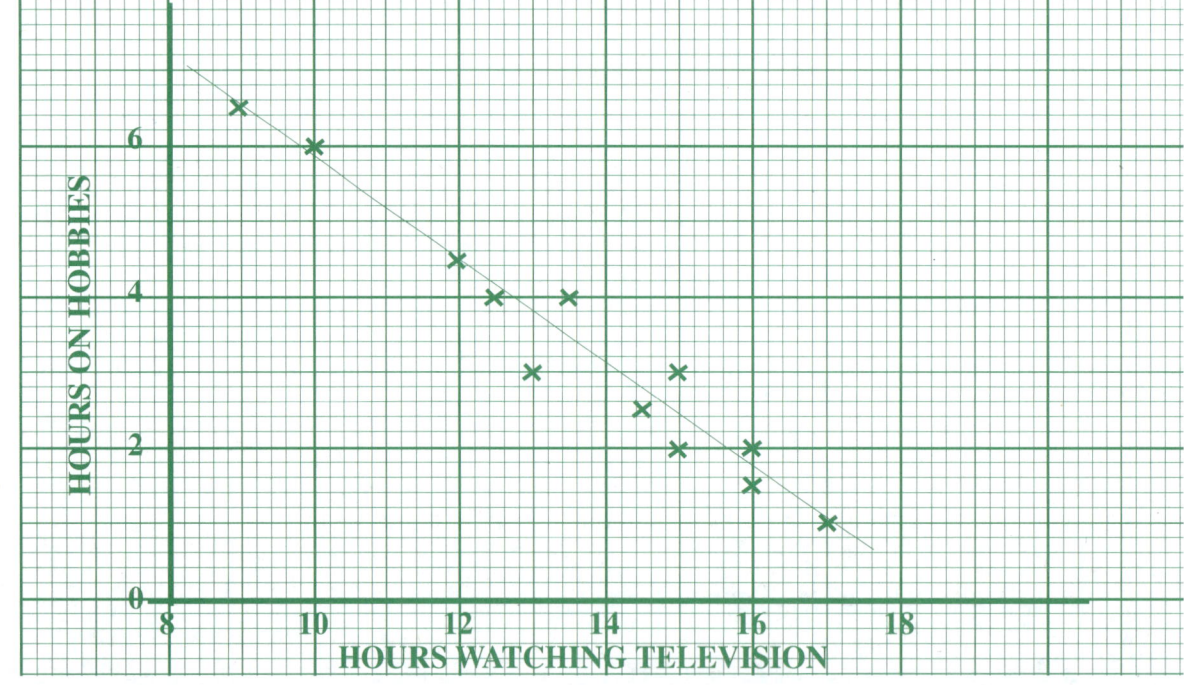

Page 26   a   A = 83°   b   B = 63°   c   C = 34°   d 180°   e 75°

          f (i) 4 triangles   (ii) 4 x 180° = 720°   (iii) 133°

Page 29   a 2·2cm, 1·1cm   b 4cm, 2cm   c 3cm, 1·5cm

Page 30   a 15cm, 16·7cm   b 42mm, 45·2mm   c 12cm, 12·6cm

Page 31   a 82·3mm   b 13·2cm   c 20·3cm   d 314·2cm^2 e 706·9m^2 f 113·1mm^2

          g 11·9m^2

Removable Answer Section

Page 32   b 1, 4, 7, …58   c 13, 14, 15, …32   d 48, 46, 44, …10   e ⁻5, 0, 5, …90

f 2n + 4   g 4n − 1   h ⁻2n + 22

Page 34   a $\begin{bmatrix} -7 \\ -4 \\ 2 \\ 8 \end{bmatrix}$ b $\begin{bmatrix} 0 \\ 4 \\ 8 \\ 10 \end{bmatrix}$ c $\begin{bmatrix} 10 \\ 6 \\ 4 \\ 0 \end{bmatrix}$ d (⁻1, ⁻7) (0, ⁻4) (2, 2) (4, 8)

e (⁻6, 0) (⁻2, 4) (2, 8) (4, 10)   f (⁻3, 10) (⁻1, 6) (0, 4) (2, 0)

Page 35   a (i) 12°   (ii) 168°   (iii) 84°   (iv) 72°   (v) 36°

b (i) red 108°, blue 63°, white 99°, green 54°, other 36°

Page 37   a 50 people   b 155 - 165   c 18 people   d
10 ≤ t < 15 |||| 5
15 ≤ t < 20 |||| 4
20 ≤ t < 25 |||| 5
25 ≤ t < 30 |||| | 6
30 ≤ t < 35 |||| ||| 8
35 ≤ t < 40 |||| || 7
40 ≤ t < 45 |||| 5
Total 40

e Yes   f 14 people   g 12 people

Page 38   a y = 2   b w = 7   c x = 2   d p = 4   e z = 12   f x = 8

Page 39   4·18   Page 40   (1) a (0, 1)   b (⁻2, ⁻3)

Page 41   (2) a (0, ⁻3)   b (4, 1)   c (⁻1, ⁻4)

(3) Any four from (⁻4, ⁻17) (⁻3, ⁻14) (⁻2, ⁻11) (⁻1, ⁻8) (0, ⁻5) (1, ⁻2) (2, 1) (3, 4) (4, 7)

(4) a 1   b ⁻3   c ⁻5   (5) 4

Page 42   (1)

	1	2	3	4	5	6
H	H1	H2	H3	H4	H5	H6
T	T1	T2	T3	T4	T5	T6

(a) $\frac{1}{12}$
(b) $\frac{3}{12}$ or $\frac{1}{4}$
(c) $\frac{2}{12}$ or $\frac{1}{6}$

(2)

	R	W	B
R	RR	RW	RB
W	WR	WW	WB
B	BR	BW	BB

(a) $\frac{3}{9}$ or $\frac{1}{3}$
(b) $\frac{6}{9}$ or $\frac{2}{3}$
(c) $\frac{5}{9}$

Removable Answer Section

Page 42 (3)

	1	2	3	4	5	6
6	7	8	9	10	11	12
5	6	7	8	9	10	11
4	5	6	7	8	9	10
3	4	5	6	7	8	9
2	3	4	5	6	7	8
1	2	3	4	5	6	7

(a) $\frac{3}{36}$ or $\frac{1}{12}$
(b) $\frac{6}{36}$ or $\frac{1}{6}$
(c) $\frac{18}{36}$ or $\frac{1}{2}$
(d) $\frac{11}{36}$

Page 43 a 25:35   b £480 : £520   c 600g : 400g   d 45° : 60° : 75°

Page 44 a 1:3   b 2:7   c 3:5   d 1:12   e 3:40   f 8:1
g 30cm   h 300g   i 5·5cm

Page 45 a $56a^7$ b $54b^{11}$ c $4c^4$ d $11d^4$ e $10e^{13}$ f $3\frac{1}{2}f^{15}$ g g^{14} h h^{12}
i i^{20} j $16j^6$ k $k^2 + 3k$ l $l^3 - 5l^2$ m $2m^4 + 10m^2$
n $30n^2 - 3n^4$ p $6p^4 - 6p^5$ q $66q^2 - 132q^3$

Page 46 a 25   b 16,000   c 25   d 9   e 27   f 125cm
g 500,062   h 108cm²   i ⁻4°C   j 0·03

Page 47 a 110°   b 5   c 23   d £6·40   e 70%   f 6200
g 48   h 36cm   i 3^9 j 30° (within 10°)

Page 48 a 15   b 26   c £14·90   d £18   e $7\frac{1}{2}$ mph   f 84   [(4 + 17) x 4]
g 20·4cm   h £72·60   i 435 mins   j 15

Removable Answer Section

Scatter Diagrams continued

The following table shows the amount of time that twelve people spend, on average, each week watching television and taking part in hobbies or interests:

Person number:	1	2	3	4	5	6	7	8	9	10	11	12
TV hours	10	12·5	13·5	17	16	9	14·5	16	15	13	15	12
Hobbies hours	6	4	4	1	1·5	6·5	2·5	2	2	3	3	4·5

(a) Plot this information on a graph using axes like these:

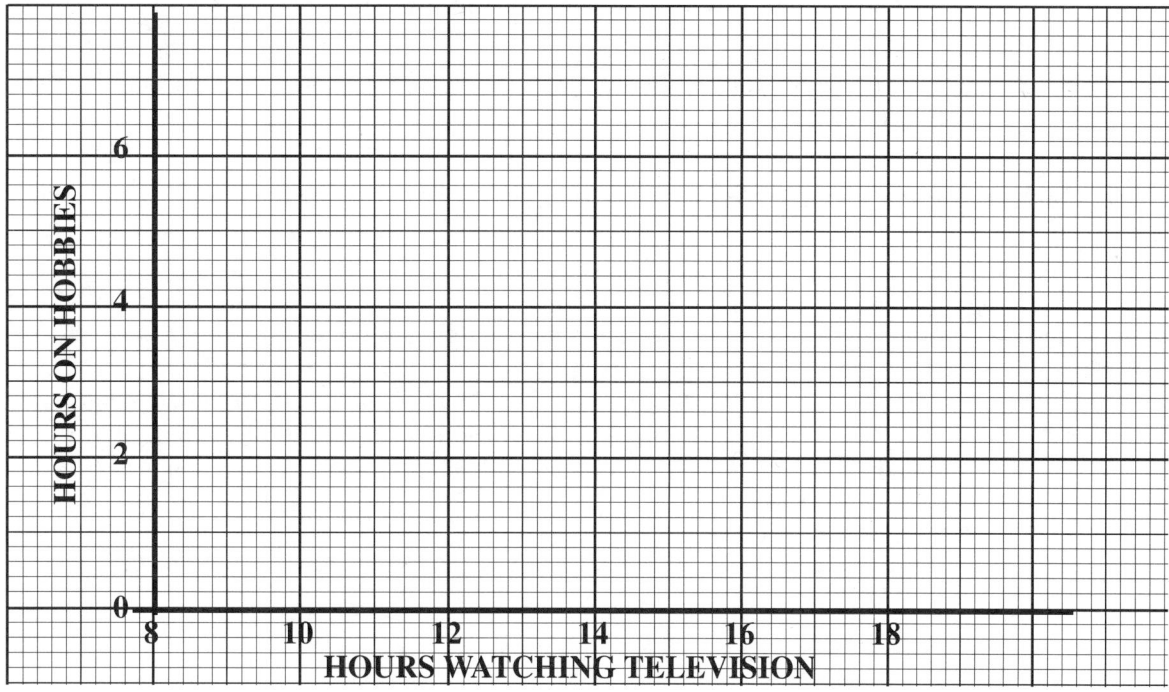

You should find that, on this graph, your points go from the top left to the bottom right.
This is because as one quantity increases the other decreases.
This is called **negative correlation.**

(b) On your graph, draw in a line of best fit.
Use it to estimate the amount of hours spent watching television by someone who spends 5 hours on hobbies.

(Your answer should be around 11·2 hours but it will depend on where your line of best fit is.)

Note: Sometimes the data which you are using gives you points on your graph which are widely spaced out.

A line cannot be put in to be near all of them ... we say that there is no correlation.

Angles in Polygons

Measure each angle in this triangle, then add the three together.

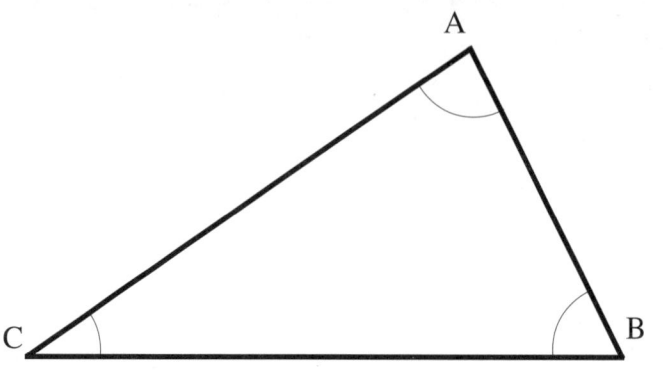

(a) ∠ A =
(b) ∠ B =
(c) ∠ C =

(d) ∠ A + ∠ B + ∠ C =

If you have measured accurately **the total of the three angles should be 180°**.

The fact that the three angles of a triangle always add up to 180° can be used to find the sum of the angles of other shapes.

Any straight-sided shape can be divided into triangles by drawing lines from just one corner to all the others.

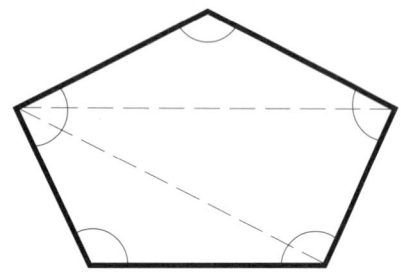

This pentagon has been divided into three triangles. The angles of the triangles when put together are the same as the angles of the pentagon. This means that **the sum of the angles of a pentagon is 3 x 180° = 540°**.

(e) Calculate the missing angle in this triangle:

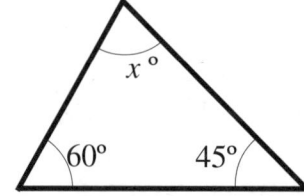

(f) (i) By drawing diagonals from corner A in this hexagon, how many triangles will it divide into?

(ii) Use your answer to part (i) to work out the sum of the six angles.

(iii) If five of the angles add up to 587° what is the size of the sixth angle?

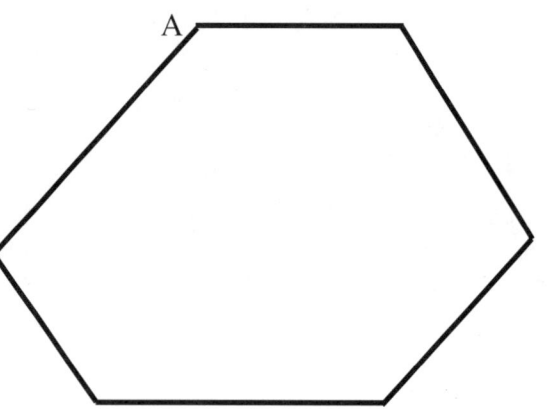

26

Enlargement

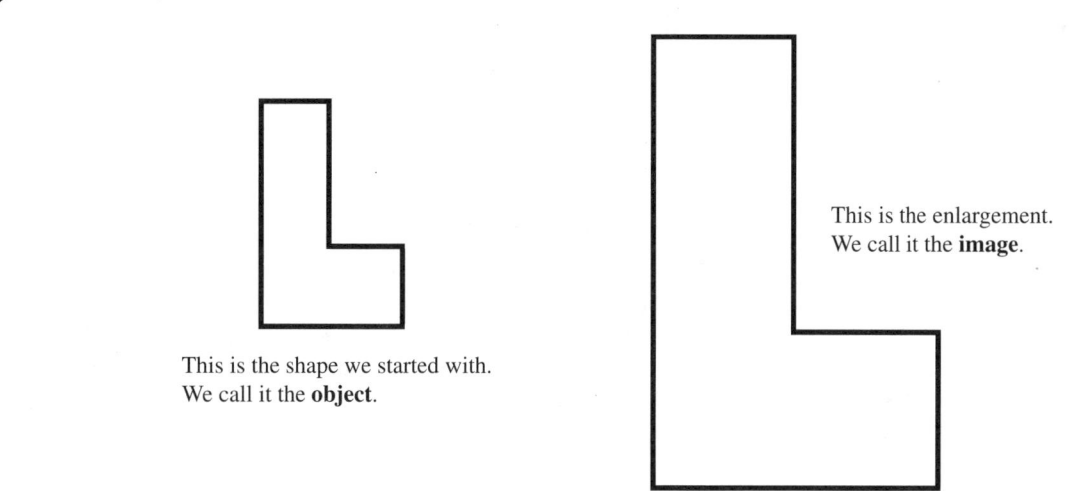

This is the shape we started with. We call it the **object**.

This is the enlargement. We call it the **image**.

The left hand shape above has been **enlarged** to make the right hand shape.

All the lengths have been doubled so we say that it has been enlarged by a **scale factor of 2**.

We can write scale factor 2 like this: **S.F. 2**

Make enlargements of these shapes, to the scale factor given.
You will need to measure each shape carefully first.

(a) S.F. 2   (b) S.F. 3   (c) S.F. 4

Sometimes a **centre of enlargement** is given. This will fix the exact position of the image.

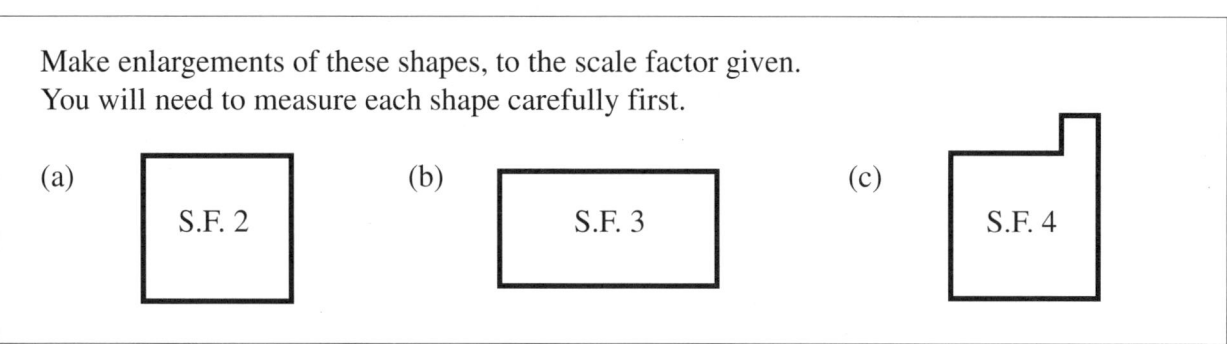

As this enlargement is to S.F. 2:

the **distance from the centre to the image** is **double** the **distance from the centre to the object**.

Note: the dotted lines help you to find the corners of the image by matching them to the corners of the object.

27

Enlargements, continued

The process of enlargement is easier if you use grid paper because you can count the number of squares which your object takes up horizontally and vertically.

If we wish to enlarge this shape by scale factor 3:

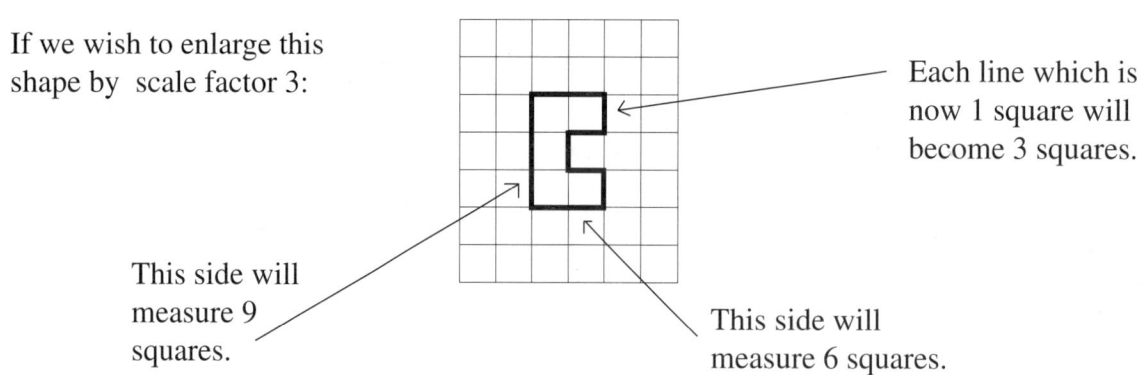

Each line which is now 1 square will become 3 squares.

This side will measure 9 squares.

This side will measure 6 squares.

In each of these examples, a centre of enlargement called *o* is used:

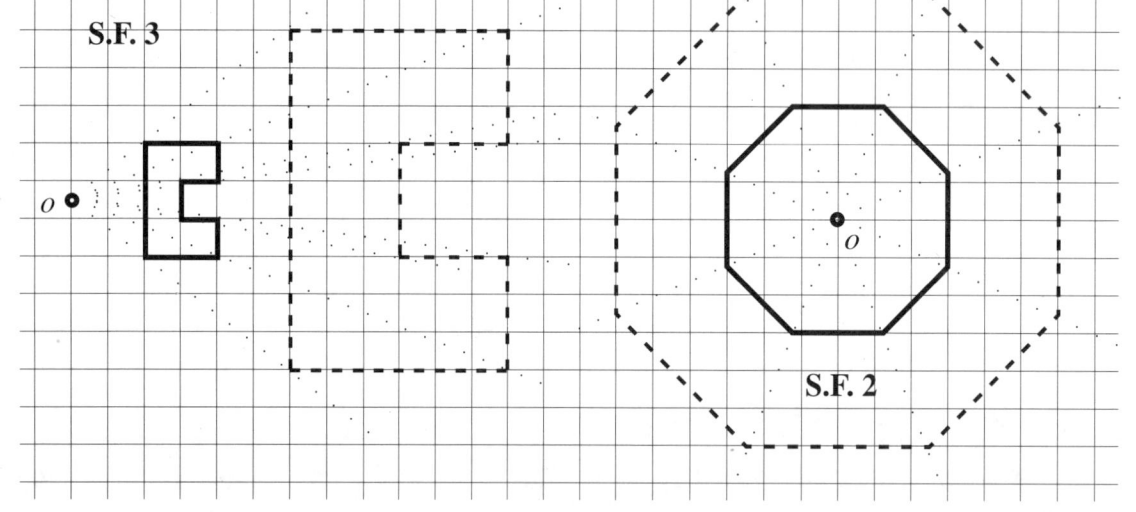

Use grid paper to make enlargements of these shapes:

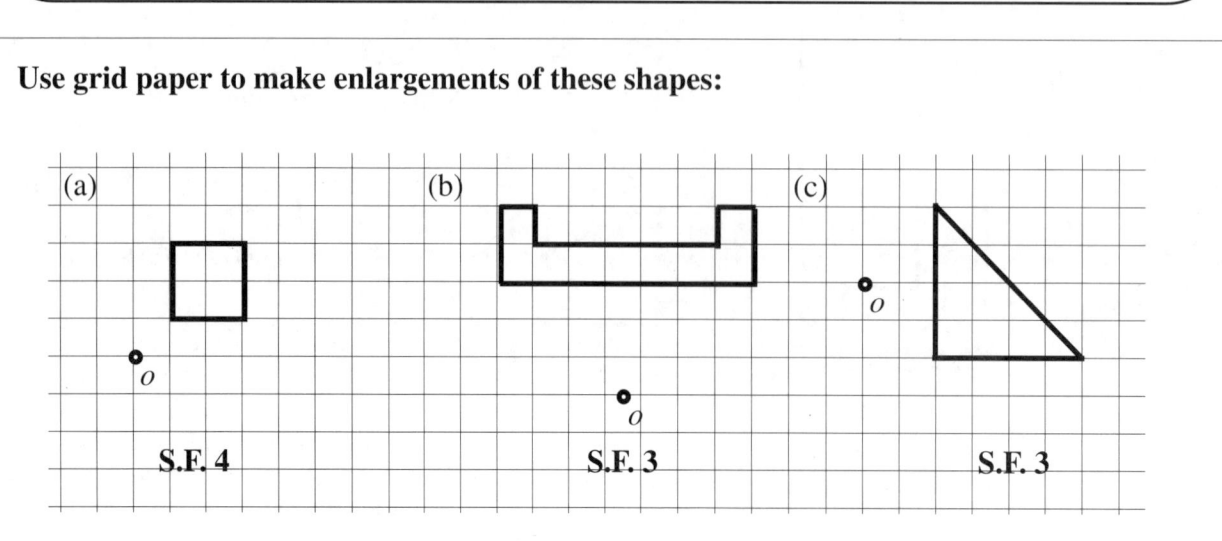

(a) S.F. 4 (b) S.F. 3 (c) S.F. 3

Circles

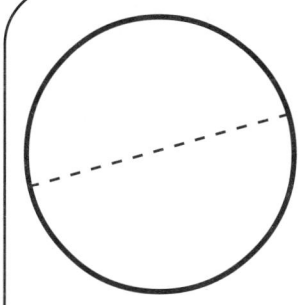

A line drawn across a circle, **passing through the centre**, is called a **diameter**.

A line drawn **from the centre to the edge** of a circle is called a **radius**.

Measure accurately the diameter and radius of each of these circles:

(a) 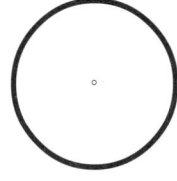　(b) 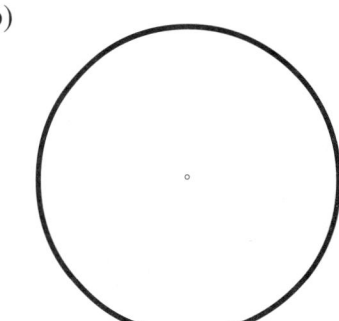　(c)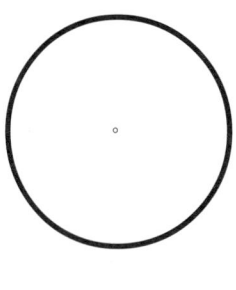

The perimeter of a circle (the distance all around it) is called its **circumference**.

The circumference of a circle is always **approximately** three times the length of its diameter.

This can be written as: $$C \approx 3 \times d$$

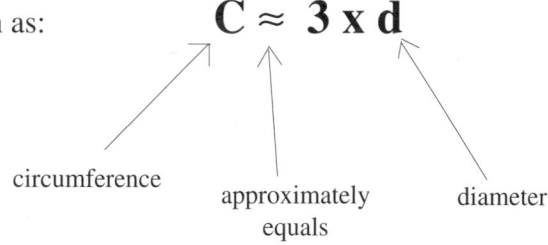

circumference　　approximately equals　　diameter

But the circumference is not exactly 3 times the diameter …

A more accurate answer is given by multiplying the diameter by a special never-ending decimal number: 3·1415 …

This number is given the Greek letter π (pi) as a name.

The value 3·142 is usually accurate enough for any calculations but it is easiest to use the π button on a scientific calculator.

29

Circles, continued

The actual formula for finding the circumference of a circle is: **C = πd**.

Another formula we can use is: **C = 2πr** where r is the radius of the circle.
(This formula works because the diameter is double the radius)

Here is an example of finding the circumference of a circle:

Firstly, as a check, we will find an approximate answer:

The diameter is roughly 12 mm.
The circumference will be approximately 3 times 12 mm.
3 x 12 mm = **36 mm**

Now we will use the formula C = 2πr:

C = 2 x π x 6·1

On a scientific calculator, we press the following keys:

| 2 | x | π | x | 6 | · | 1 | = |

… and we find the answer 38.3, to one decimal place.

(Note: on some calculators the yellow, 2nd function, button will need to be pressed before pressing the π button)

**Find the circumferences of the following circles giving your answers to 1 d.p.
Give an estimate first and also write down what you put into the calculator.**

(a)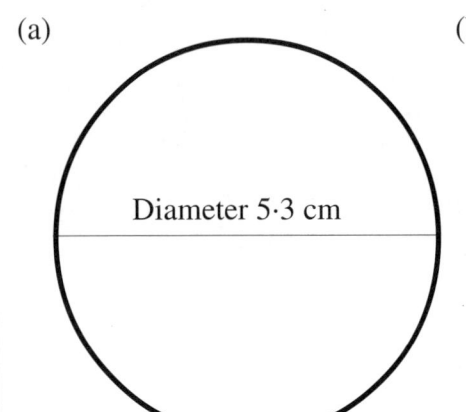
Diameter 5·3 cm

(b)
7·2 mm

(c)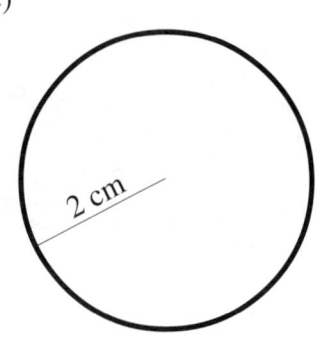
2 cm

30

Even More Circles

This is a semi-circle with a diameter of 6 cm.

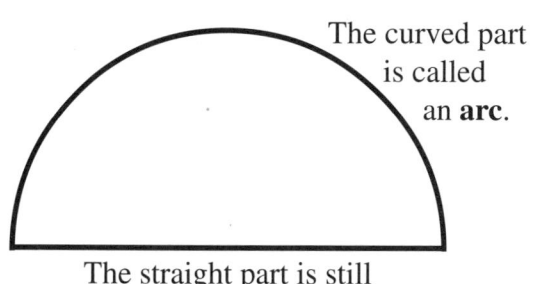

The curved part is called an **arc**.

The straight part is still called the diameter.

The perimeter of the semi-circle can be found by working out the length of the arc and adding on the length of the diameter. If this was a whole circle, the circumference would be found by calculating $\pi \times 6$. Obviously the length of the arc is half of that.

Length of arc = $\frac{1}{2} \times \pi \times 6 = 9.4$ (to 1 d.p.)
Length of diameter = 6
Total perimeter = 15.4 cm

Find the perimeters of these shapes:

(a)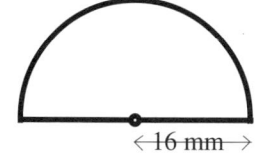
16 mm

(b)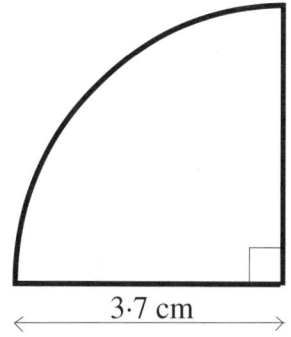
3.7 cm

(c) 5 cm, 4 cm

The area of a circle can be found using the formula $A = \pi r^2$

6.1 mm

Using the same circle as before:

An estimate of the area is $3 \times 6^2 = 3 \times 36$
$= 108$ mm^2

The actual area is $\pi \times 6.1^2 = 116.9$ mm^2 (to 1 d.p.)

Find the areas of the circles described:

(d) A circle of radius 10 cm

(e) A circle of radius 15 m

(f) A circle of diameter 12 mm

(g) A circle of diameter 3.9 m

Linear Patterns

A sequence of numbers can be given by a mathematical rule:

For example: nth term $= 3n + 2$ (which means 3 x n add 2)

So ...   if $n = 1$ 1st term $= 3 \times 1 + 2 = $ **5**
if $n = 2$ 2nd term $= 3 \times 2 + 2 = $ **8**
if $n = 3$ 3rd term $= 3 \times 3 + 2 = $ **11**
or   if $n = 100$ 100th term $= 3 \times 100 + 2 = $ **302**

Notice from the first three terms, the sequence goes up 3 each time.
This matches the ' 3 ' in the rule **3n + 2**.

Find the first 3 terms and the 20th term for these sequences:
(The first one has been done for you)

(a) nth term $= 4n + 1$ 1st $= 4 \times 1 + 1 = 5$ 2nd $= 4 \times 2 + 1 = 9$
3rd $= 4 \times 3 + 1 = 13$ 20th $= 4 \times 20 + 1 = 81$

(b) nth term $= 3n - 2$

(c) nth term $= n + 12$

(d) nth term $= 50 - 2n$

(e) nth term $= 5n - 10$

If you know the sequence and want to find the nth term, first work out the **constant** difference.

Look at this sequence: **7   9   11   13   ...**

The difference between the numbers is 2, so the nth term has **2n** in it ... but $2 \times 1 = $ **2**
$2 \times 2 = $ **4**
$2 \times 3 = $ **6**
$2 \times 4 = $ **8**

Each of these answers is **5** less than the corresponding number in the sequence   7, 9, 11, 13 ...

So the nth term is   **2n + 5**   (the 5 is called the **constant**)

Find the nth term for these sequences:

(f)   6, 8, 10, 12 ...   (g)   3, 7, 11, 15 ...   (h)   20, 18, 16, 14 ...

Mappings

Mappings represent rules in a similar way to linear patterns which were shown on page 32. Mappings are usually given in diagram form and the resulting pairs of numbers can be plotted on a graph.

The diagram below shows the mapping $x \rightarrow 2x - 1$

$$x \rightarrow 2x - 1$$

$$\begin{pmatrix} 1 \\ 3 \\ 5 \\ 7 \end{pmatrix} \longrightarrow \begin{pmatrix} 1 \\ 5 \\ 9 \\ 13 \end{pmatrix}$$

This side of the mapping can show any value of x that we choose.

This side of the mapping shows what happens when you use the formula

$$x \rightarrow 2x - 1.$$

For example, when we chose a value for x of 5, we had to use the formula to find out what went on the right-hand side of the mapping:

$2x - 1$ becomes $2 \times 5 - 1$.
$2 \times 5 - 1 = 9$

$x \rightarrow 2x - 1$

$$\begin{pmatrix} 1 \\ 3 \\ 5 \\ 7 \end{pmatrix} \longrightarrow \begin{pmatrix} 1 \\ 5 \\ 9 \\ 13 \end{pmatrix}$$

If the pairs of numbers are written as coordinates (1,1) (3,5) (5,9) (7,13) they can be plotted and connected. The graph can then be used to find any other pairs which follow the rule $x \rightarrow 2x - 1$. For example, when $x = 6$ $y = 11$.

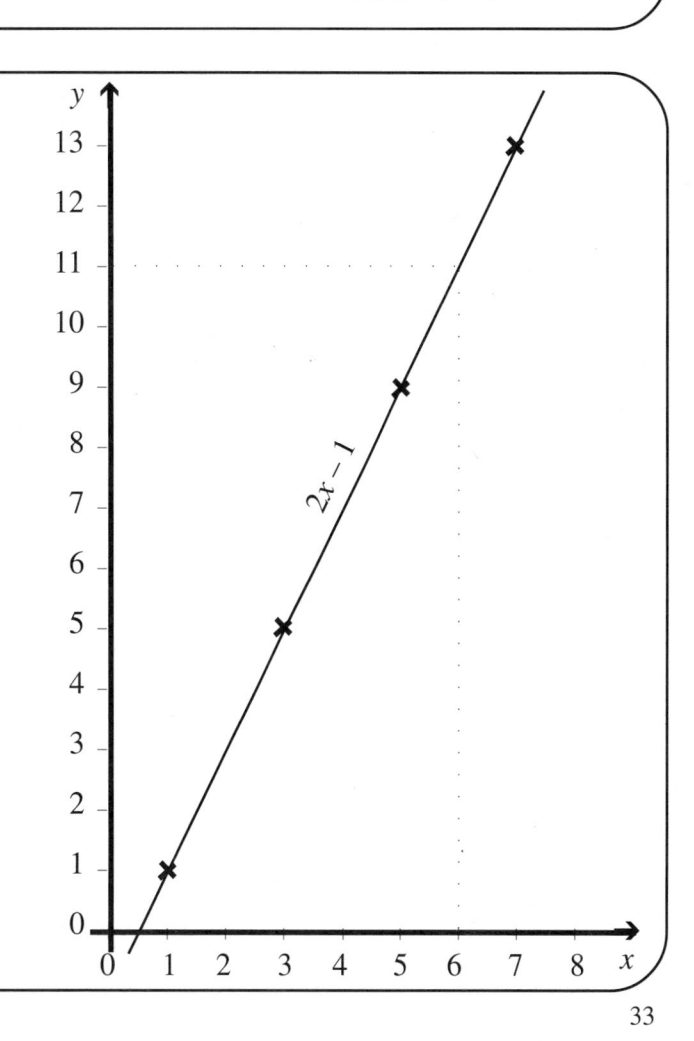

33

Mappings, continued

Copy and complete these three mapping diagrams:

(a) $x \rightarrow 3x - 4$

$^-1 \rightarrow$
$0 \rightarrow ^-4$
$2 \rightarrow$
$4 \rightarrow$

(b) $x \rightarrow x + 6$

$^-6 \rightarrow$
$^-2 \rightarrow$
$2 \rightarrow$
$4 \rightarrow 10$

(c) $x \rightarrow 4 - 2x$

$^-3 \rightarrow 10$
$^-1 \rightarrow$
$0 \rightarrow$
$2 \rightarrow$

List the coordinates for each of the mapping diagrams:

(d) The coordinates for the diagram in question (a) are: ($^-1$,) (0, $^-4$) (2,) (4,)

(e) The coordinates for the diagram in question (b) are: ($^-6$,) ($^-2$,) (2,) (4, 10)

(f) The coordinates for the diagram in question (c) are: ($^-3$, 10) ($^-1$,) (0,) (2,)

Now make a copy of the axes shown below.
Plot the coordinates and draw the connecting line for each of the mappings.

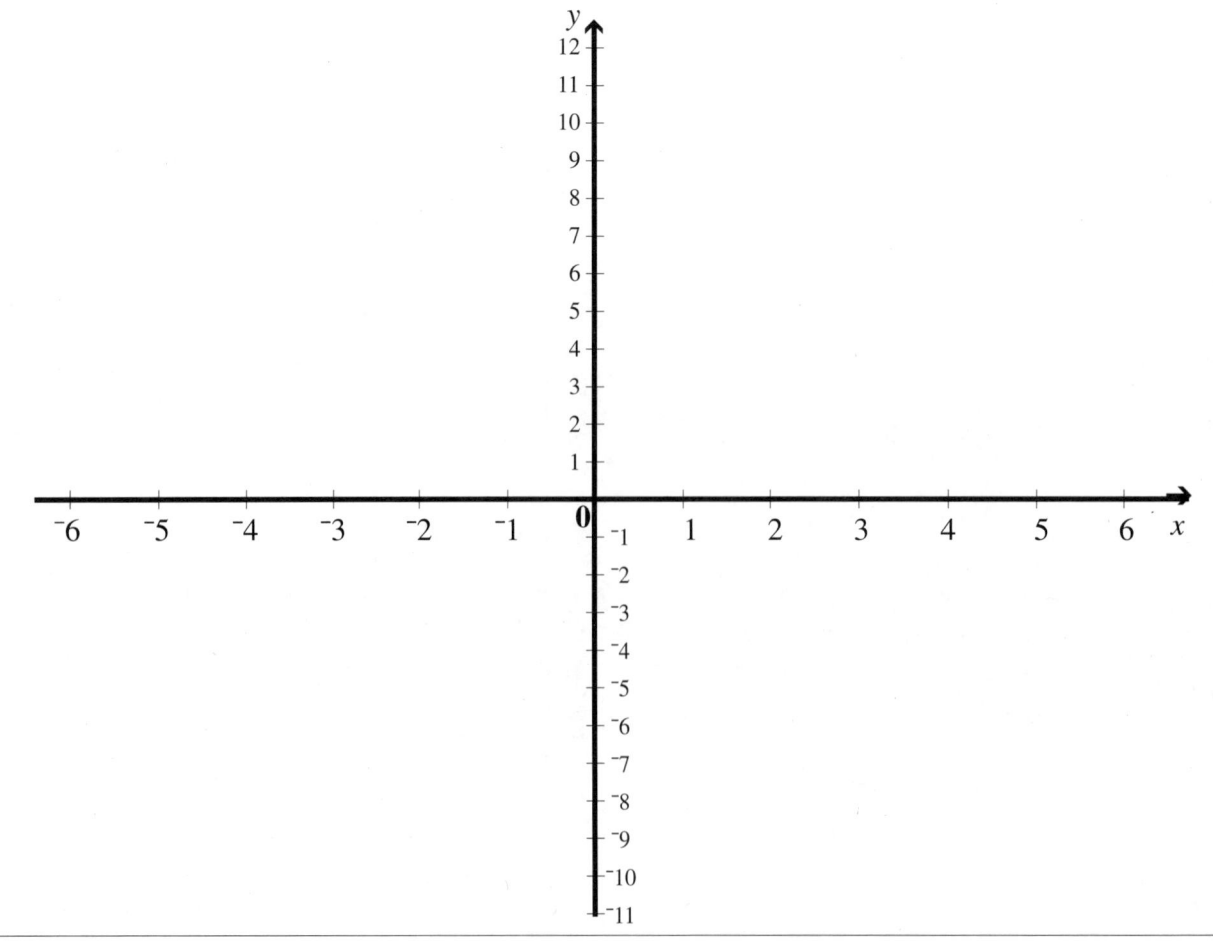

34

Pie Charts

Example: In a survey of 20 people, 11 were wearing brown shoes, 5 were wearing black shoes and 4 had shoes of a different colour. To show this on a pie chart we must first work out how many degrees represent 1 person:

20 people are represented by the whole 'pie' = 360°

1 person must be represented by 18°   (360° ÷ 20)

… so the size of the sector to represent: brown shoes is   11 x 18° = 198°
black shoes is   5 x 18° = 90°
other colours is   4 x 18° = 72°
Total   = 360°

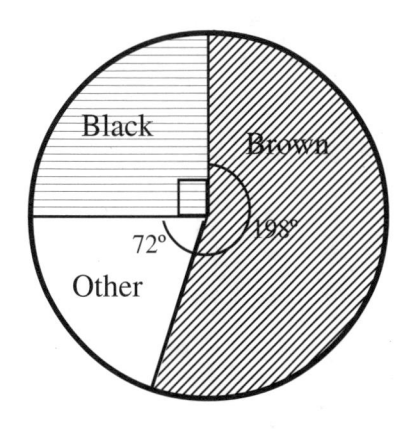

For both sets of data below, work out the angles required to create a pie-chart. Draw the pie-chart for each set of data.

(a)   30 people were asked how they travelled to school:

14 said they walked   7 travelled by car   6 travelled by bus   3 cycled

(i)   What angle would represent 1 person?
(ii) What angle would represent the people who walked?
(iii) What angle would represent the people who travelled by car?
(iv) What angle would represent the people who travelled by bus?
(v)   What angle would represent the people who cycled?
(vi) Draw the pie-chart.

(b)   In a traffic survey, the colour of each car was noted as it passed the school gate:

12 were red   7 were blue   11 were white   6 were green   4 were other colours

Work out the angles required and show this information in a pie-chart.

Class Intervals

When collecting a large amount of data,
it is best to group it together so that it is easier to understand:

The heights (in cm) of some 13 year-olds are shown in this table:

```
160  141  171  179  148  178  159  173  165  162
166  165  161  148  138  181  147  148  158  152
149  162  156  154  160  150  139  166  153  140
159  176  159  168  150  169  179  161  151  169
167  143  178  158  171  140  153  177  163  161
```

We can begin to group this together by, for example, counting the number of people whose height is equal to or more than 135 cm but less than 145 cm:

```
160  **141**  171  179  148  178  159  173  165  162
166  165  161  148  **138**  181  147  148  158  152
149  162  156  154  160  150  **139**  166  153  **140**
159  176  159  168  150  169  179  161  151  169
167  **143**  178  158  171  **140**  153  177  163  161
```

We can say that we are looking at an **interval** of: $135 \leq h < 145$

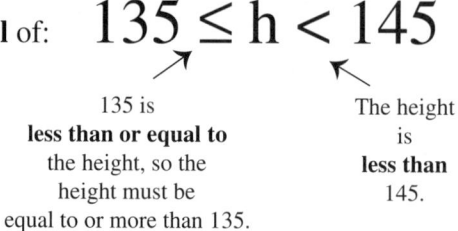

135 is **less than or equal to** the height, so the height must be equal to or more than 135.

The height is **less than** 145.

There are 6 people who fit this interval.
We say that there is a **frequency** of 6 for this interval.

Now consider the other intervals:

$145 \leq h < 155$

The height is equal to or more than 145 cm but it is less than 155 cm.

$155 \leq h < 165$

The height is equal to or more than 155 cm but it is less than 165 cm.

$165 \leq h < 175$

The height is equal to or more than 165 cm but it is less than 175 cm.

$175 \leq h < 185$

The height is equal to or more than 175 cm but it is less than 185 cm.

Using these intervals we create a **frequency table**:

interval	frequency
$135 \leq h < 145$	6
$145 \leq h < 155$	12
$155 \leq h < 165$	14
$165 \leq h < 175$	11
$175 \leq h < 185$	7
	50

Class Intervals, continued

Answer these questions about the data regarding heights of 13 year-olds.

Use the frequency table to help you.

(a) How many people were measured?

(b) Which height interval was most common?

(c) How many people were at least 165 cm tall?

A large group of people decided to do a maths puzzle.
Here is a set of data about the time taken to complete it.
The time is shown in seconds.

40	17	30	39	34	35	39	22	13	33
20	26	21	15	35	28	20	37	19	25
14	32	10	26	43	32	14	26	22	30
34	38	40	31	15	40	12	36	29	41

(d) Use the data to complete this frequency table:

time	frequency
$10 \leq t < 15$	
$15 \leq t < 20$	
$20 \leq t < 25$	
$25 \leq t < 30$	
$30 \leq t < 35$	
$35 \leq t < 40$	
$40 \leq t < 45$	
Total	

(e) Does the total at the bottom of the frequency table match the number of pieces of data?

(f) How many people took less than 25 seconds to do the puzzle?

(g) How many people took more than 35 seconds to do the puzzle?

Trial and Improvement

If you look back at page 18 you will remember that we sometimes try to find the value of x when we look at equations:

For example to solve $2x + 4 = 10$ we first subtract 4 from both sides
$2x = 6$ now we divide both sides by 2
… and we have the answer: $x = 3$

Find the value of the letter in each of these equations:

(a) $y + 6 = 8$ (b) $2w - 4 = 10$ (c) $3x + 4 = 12 - x$

(d) $5p = 20$ (e) $\dfrac{z}{4} = 3$ (f) $2x - 9 = 7$

Some equations are too difficult, at this stage, to calculate an answer …

… with the aid of a calculator an approximate answer can be found.

For example, suppose we wish to find the value of x in this equation: $x^2 + 2x = 20$

We could try $x = 1$ to see if it works: $1^2 + 2 \times 1 = 3$ (3 is too small …
… we want 20)

Try $x = 2$: $2^2 + 2 \times 2 = 8$ (8 is too small)
Try $x = 3$: $3^2 + 2 \times 3 = 15$ (15 is too small)
Try $x = 4$: $4^2 + 2 \times 4 = 24$ (24 is too big)

$x = 3$ gives a result which is too small and $x = 4$ gives a result which is too big so the actual answer is **between 3 and 4**.

Now try values of x between 3 and 4 that have one decimal place:

Try $x = 3.5$: $3.5^2 + 2 \times 3.5 = 19.25$ (too small)
Try $x = 3.6$: $3.6^2 + 2 \times 3.6 = 20.16$ (too big)

… so the actual answer must be **between 3·5 and 3·6**.

Trial and Improvement, continued

... Continuing from page 38:

We know that the value of x lies between 3·5 and 3·6.
If a more accurate answer is needed we can use the calculator to try possible values of x between 3·5 and 3·6 which have two decimal places:

   Try $x = 3·55$: $3·55^2 + 2 \times 3·55 = 19·7025$ (too small)

   Try $x = 3·56$: $3·56^2 + 2 \times 3·56 = 19·7936$ (too small)

   Try $x = 3·57$: $3·57^2 + 2 \times 3·57 = 19·8849$ (too small)

   Try $x = 3·58$: $3·58^2 + 2 \times 3·58 = 19·9764$ (too small)

   Try $x = 3·59$: $3·59^2 + 2 \times 3·59 = 20·0681$ (too big)

... so the actual value of x lies between 3·58 and 3·59.

If we want to find an answer to **two** decimal places we can't choose 3·58 or 3·59 unless we try some possible values of x which have **three** decimal places:

   Try $x = 3·584$: $3·584^2 + 2 \times 3·584 = 20·013056$

... this answer is still slightly too big, so the value of x must be between 3·580 and 3·584.

Both of these would round to 3·58 so at last we can say:

$$x = 3·58 \text{ to 2 d.p.}$$

Use the method of trial and improvement to solve the equation below.
Give your answer to two decimal places.
The process has been started for you.

$$x^2 + 3x = 30$$

   Try $x = 2$ $2^2 + 3 \times 2 = 10$ (too small)

   Try $x = 3$ $3^2 + 3 \times 3 = 18$ (too small)

   Try $x = 4$ $4^2 + 3 \times 4 = \ldots$

   Try $x = 5$ ...

Equations of Lines

Equations of lines are very similar to mappings.

$y = 2x + 1$ is an equation which connects two numbers, an *x* number and a *y* number:

if $x = 1$ ...the value of *y* is $2 \times 1 + 1 = 3$

if $x = 4$ ...the value of *y* is $2 \times 4 + 1 = 9$

Each pair of numbers can be written as a coordinate (x, y)
... so the two pairs so far are **(1, 3)** and **(4, 9)**.

Now answer these questions:

(1) For the equation, $y = 2x + 1$ we have found the coordinates (1, 3) and (4, 9).

Using the same equation, $y = 2x + 1$, complete
these coordinates by filling in the missing numbers: (a) (0,)   (b) (⁻2,)

(c) On a piece of graph paper, draw axes like the ones in the diagram below.
Plot the four points and join them with a straight line.
The line should continue at both ends, to the edges of the paper.

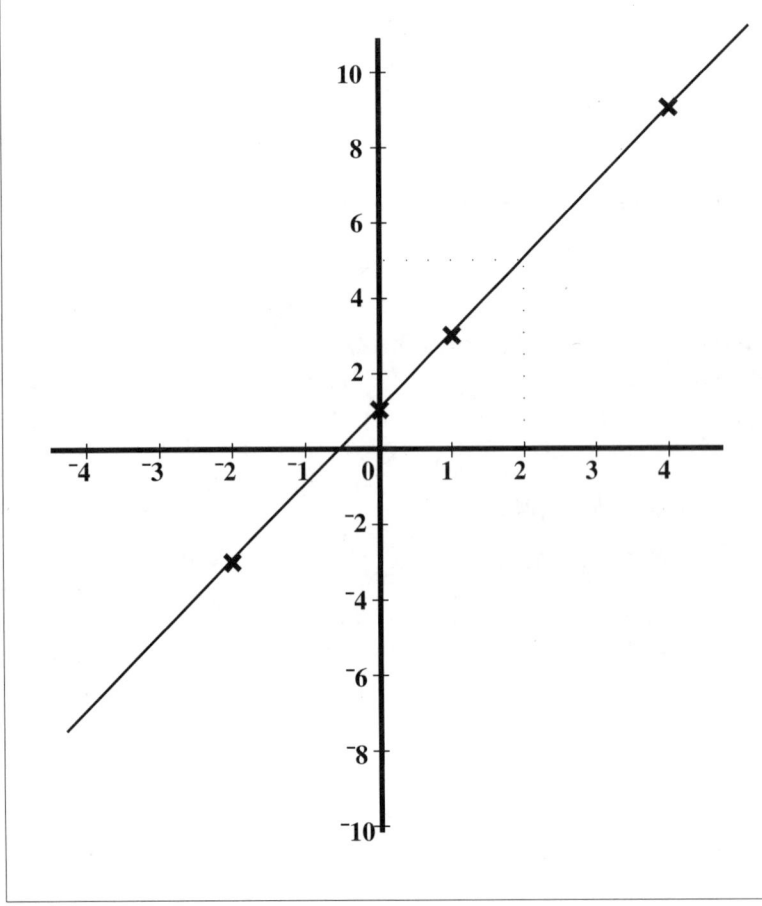

Two points would have been enough to be able to draw the line, but it is always better to find three or four points just in case you make a mistake with a coordinate.

Notice that all the points that lie on the line, e.g. (2, 5), obey the rule "the *y* number is equal to double the *x* number plus 1."

Equations of Lines, continued

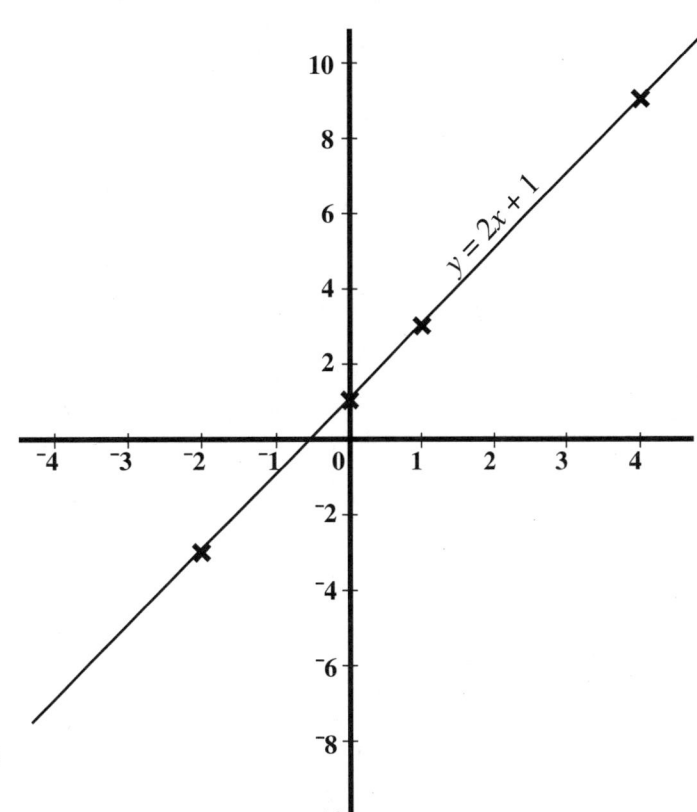

Use the same graph which you used for question 1 on page 40 to plot the lines in the following questions.

(2) Using the equation $y = x - 3$ complete the following coordinates. The first one has been done for you.

(1, ⁻2)   (a) (0,)   (b) (4,)   (c) (⁻1,)

(d) Plot these four points on the same graph as question 1. Join the points with a straight line and label it $y = x - 3$.

(3) (a) Write down the coordinates of four points that are on the line $y = 3x - 5$. (Start by choosing an x number and then working out the y number that goes with it.)

(b) Plot the four points on the same graph as before. If any of the points does not fit, don't worry work out another that does. Join the points with a straight line and label it $y = 3x - 5$.

(4) Write down the number on the y axis where each line crosses:

(a) $y = 2x + 1$ crosses the y axis at …

(b) $y = x - 3$ crosses the y axis at …

(c) $y = 3x - 5$ crosses the y axis at …

(5) Write down the number on the y axis where the line $y = 2x + 4$ will cross.

Probability Again

If two coins are spun it is easiest to show all the possible outcomes in a table:

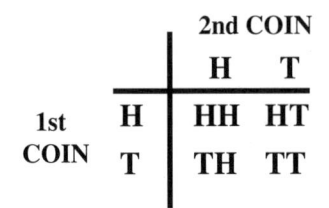

	2nd COIN	
1st COIN	H	T
H	HH	HT
T	TH	TT

You can see from the table that there are four possible outcomes. A table which shows all possible outcomes is called a **possibility space**.

Using the notation P( ) as short for "the probability of":

... P(two heads) = $\frac{1}{4}$ P(one of each) = $\frac{2}{4}$ = $\frac{1}{2}$

Now answer these questions:

(1) Copy and complete this table to show all the possible outcomes of spinning a coin and rolling a die:

	DIE					
COIN	1	2	3	4	5	6
H	H1					
T			T3			

Find:
(a) P(a head and a six)
(b) P(a tail and an odd number)
(c) P(a head and a multiple of 3)

(2) Two bags each contain a Red, a White and a Blue counter.
A counter is taken from each bag.
Copy and complete the following possibility space:

	2nd BAG		
1st BAG	R	W	B
R	RR		
W			
B		BW	

Find:
(a) P(both the same colour)
(b) P(two different colours)
(c) P(at least one counter is blue)

(3) Copy and complete the table below to show all the outcomes for two dice being rolled **and** their numbers being added together:

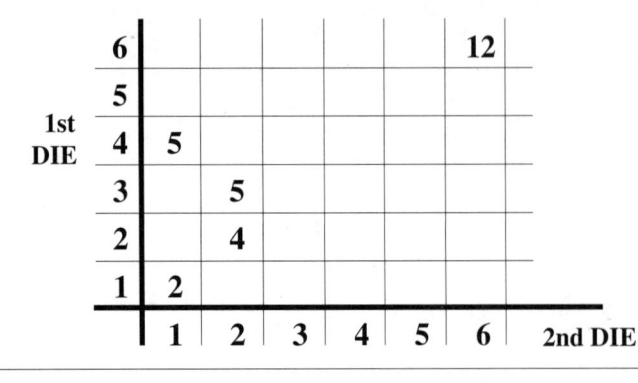

1st DIE
6						12
5						
4	5					
3		5				
2		4				
1	2					
	1	2	3	4	5	6

2nd DIE

Find:
(a) P(4)
(b) P(7)
(c) P(an even score)
(d) P(at least one six)

More ratio

A 10 cm line is to be cut in the ratio **2:3**.

This can be thought of as cutting the line into **5** parts as 2 + 3 = 5

   ... so each part is 2cm long because 10cm ÷ 5 = 2cm.

2 : 3

The piece on the left is 2 x 2cm = 4cm.   The piece on the right is 3 x 2cm = 6cm.

(As a check, add the two answers to make sure that all 10 centimetres have been used.)

We can say:

"When a 10cm line is cut in the ratio 2:3, one piece will be 4cm the other will be 6cm."

We would write the answer simply like this: **4cm, 6cm.**

Now try these:

(a)   Divide 60 in the ratio 5:7. (remember to add the 5 and 7 together first)

(b)   Two people are to share £1000 in the ratio of their ages.
      If one person is 12 and the other is 13, how much does each get?

(c)   1kg of brass is made by mixing copper and zinc in the ratio 60%:40%.
      How many grams of copper and zinc are needed?

(d)   The angles of a triangle are in the ratio 3:4:5.
      What is the size of each angle?

In question (c) above, the ratio 60%:40% could be **cancelled down** to a simpler form by **dividing both numbers by the same amount**:

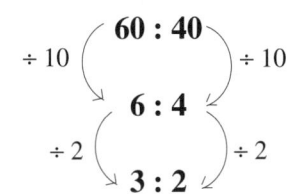

60 : 40
÷ 10   ÷ 10
6 : 4
÷ 2   ÷ 2
3 : 2

When the two numbers will no longer divide to produce whole numbers, the ratio is in its simplest form ...

... so the ratio 60:40 can be expressed as the ratio 3:2.

Ratio continued

When simplifying a ratio always make sure that you are cancelling amounts that have the same units:

the ratio of **30 minutes : 2 hours**

should first be changed to: **30 minutes : 120 minutes**

This can then be simplified: **30 minutes : 120 minutes**

÷ 30 → **1 : 4** ← ÷ 30

The final ratio 1 : 4 does not need units.
The ratio simply tells you that the second quantity is four times the size of the first quantity.

Cancel the following ratios to their simplest forms:

(a) 16 : 48 (b) 16 : 56 (c) 21 : 35

(d) 15 mins : 3 hrs (e) 15mm : 20cm (f) 1 kg : 125 g

A quantity can be increased (or decreased) by a given ratio:

Suppose a photograph that is 6 inches long and 4 inches wide is to be enlarged so that the new length is 10 inches. By comparing the lengths we see that the ratio of the two photographs is 10 : 6, which can be simplified to **5 : 3** ... so the old width will be increased by the ratio 5 : 3.

New width = $\frac{5}{3}$ × 4 inches = $6\frac{2}{3}$ inches.

There are three ways of working this out:

(i) $\frac{1}{3}$ of 4 is $1\frac{1}{3}$ inches so $\frac{5}{3}$ of 4 is 5 × $1\frac{1}{3}$ = $6\frac{2}{3}$ inches.

(ii) on a calculator with a fraction button (5)($a^b/_c$)(3)(×)(4) = $6\frac{2}{3}$

(iii) on a calculator without a fraction button (5)(÷)(3)(×)(4) = 6·6̇

Now try the following questions:

(g) Find the new length of a picture that is originally 12cm long and is then enlarged in the ratio 5 : 2.

(h) A recipe for six people requires 225g of flour. How much is needed for eight people?

(i) A scale model is made of a car, with the size reduced in the ratio 1 : 72. What will be the length of the model if the real car is 3·96m long?

More algebra

You have already seen the first two rules of **indices** used with **numbers**:

For example: $2^2 \times 2^3 = 2^5$ and $3^6 \div 3^4 = 3^2$

The same rules can be applied to **letters**: $x^2 \times x^3 = x^5$ and $y^6 \div y^4 = y^2$

Now consider a mixture of numbers and letters:

$4x^2 \times 3x^3$ is short for **4 × x x × 3 × x x x**

As multiplication can be done in any order, this is the same as: **4 × 3 × x x × x x x**

… and this equals **12 x^5**   (2 + 3)

(4 × 3)

It can be seen from this that the ordinary numbers have been multiplied in the normal way. The index numbers have been added so the first law of index numbers still holds.

Similarly for a divide sum, the ordinary numbers will be divided and the index numbers will be subtracted:

For example: $12x^5 \div 3x^3 = 4x^2$ (5 – 3)

(12 ÷ 3)

Now try these:

(a) $7a^5 \times 8a^2$
(b) $6b^7 \times 9b^4$
(c) $32c^6 \div 8c^2$
(d) $121d^{11} \div 11d^7$

(e) $4e^8 \times 2\frac{1}{2}e^5$
(f) $7f^{20} \div 2f^5$
(g) $(g^7)^2$ clue: this means $g^7 \times g^7$

(h) $(h^4)^3$ clue: this means $h^4 \times h^4 \times h^4$
(i) $(i^5)^4$
(j) $(4j^3)^2$

Note: questions (g), (h) and (i) show the third rule of index numbers: $(g^7)^2$ simplifies to g^{14}

Notice that the index numbers 7 and 2 are multiplied together to give 14.

Use the methods above, together with the bracket work on page 13 to multiply out the following:

(k) $k(k + 3)$
(l) $l^2(l - 5)$
(k) $2m(m^3 + 5m)$

(k) $3n^2(10 - n^2)$
(k) $6p^3(p - p^2)$
(k) $11q(6q - 12q^2)$

MENTAL ARITHMETIC PRACTICE

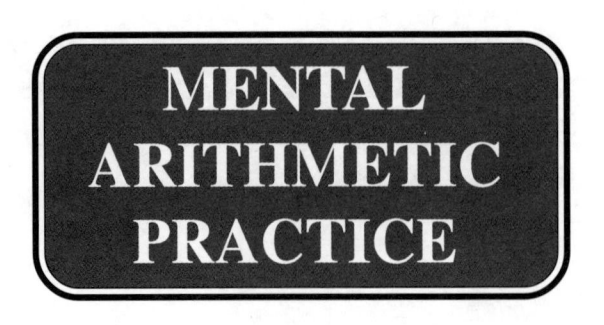

You may be given mental arithemtic tests where you are not allowed to use a calculator or to write down any working out. Although most of the questions may be quite easy, the difficulty comes with the time limits imposed. You may find that for some questions you have only 15, 10 or even 5 seconds to answer the question before the next question is read out. To help you to gain confidence we have included 30 practice questions below.

To have the best possible practice it would be best to ask someone to read each question twice, leaving the required time between questions. Alternatively, you could set a time limit of 15 minutes to try all the 30 questions.

MENTAL ARITHMETIC PRACTICE   SECTION 1

For this group of questions you should have only **5 seconds** to work out each answer.

(a) What is the next number in the sequence   1, 4, 9, 16, ...?

(b) Write down the answer to 16 multiplied by 1000.

(c) Subtract 17 from 42.

(d) What is the square root of 81?

(e) What is the value of 3 cubed?

(f) Change one and a quarter metres into centimetres.

(g) Write the number *five hundred thousand and sixty-two* in figures.

(h) What is the area of a rectangle of length 12cm and width 9cm?

(i) If the afternoon temperature of 6°C falls by 10°C during the night, what is the night time temperature?

(j) Write three hundredths as a decimal.

MENTAL ARITHMETIC PRACTICE

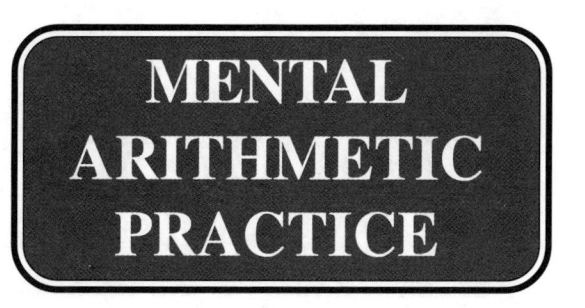

MENTAL ARITHMETIC PRACTICE   SECTION 2

For this group of questions you should have only **10 seconds** to work out each answer.

(a) Two angles of a triangle are 30° and 40°.
     What is the size of the third angle?

(b) How many different factors has the number 16 got?

(c) What is the next prime number after 19?

(d) How much is two thirds of £9.60?

(e) A person achieves a mark of seven out of ten in a test.
     What percentage is this?

(f) Multiply 6·2 by one thousand.

(g) Using the equation $y = 3x^2$ find the value of y when x is 4.

(h) Estimate the circumference of a circle with radius 6cm.

(i) Write down in index form the answer to:
     three to the power four multiplied by three to the power five.

(j) Estimate the size of the angle shown:

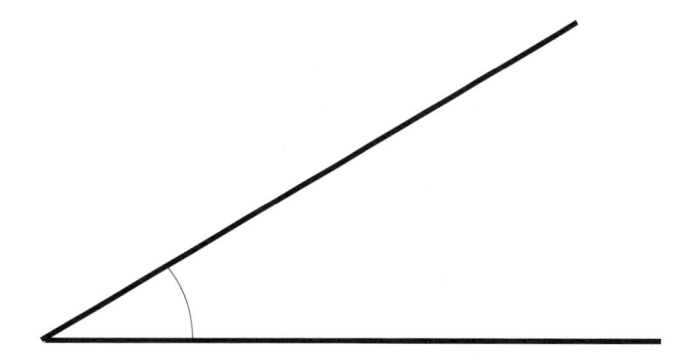

MENTAL ARITHMETIC PRACTICE

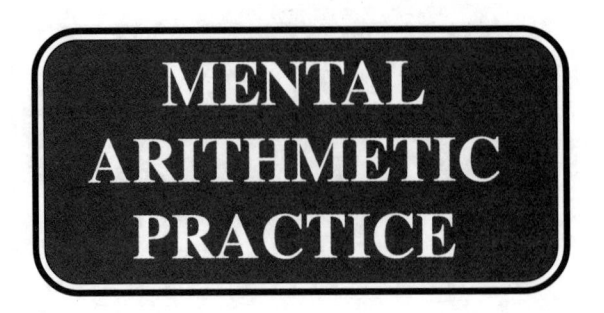

MENTAL ARITHMETIC PRACTICE   SECTION 3

For this group of questions you should have only **15 seconds** to work out each answer.

(a)   Two fifths of a number is 6. What is the number?

(b)   The *n*th term of a sequence is $3n + 2$. What is the 8th term?

(c)   What is the cost of five books at two pounds ninety-eight pence each?

(d)   Twenty-four pounds is divided in the ratio one to three.
      What is the value of the larger share?

(e)   If Alex jogs two and a half miles in twenty minutes,
      what is Alex's average speed in miles per hour?

(f)   Write an approximate answer to the following calculation:

$$(3·9 + 16·95) \times 4·1$$

(g)   What is the perimeter of a rectangle with length 6·1cm and width 4·1cm?

(h)   Increase sixty-six pounds by ten percent.

(i)   How many minutes are there in seven and a quarter hours?

(j)   What number is halfway between nine and twenty-one?

If you found the questions easy, well done!

If you found them difficult, don't worry. Look through them again <u>slowly</u> and try to solve them in your own time. You will probably be able to do most of them and the practice will help you to get used to the way that test questions are worded.